- *Simplify the Business Planning Process*
- *Create a Plan That Grows With Your Business*
- *Tailor a Plan to Your Company*
- *Develop A Quick-Hitting Set of Priorities*
- *Avoid Business Mistakes and Pitfalls*
- *Simplify An Overwhelming Process*
- *Build As Your Business Develops*
- *Demystify the Business Planning Process*
- *Ignore Traditional Cookie-Cutter Plans*
- *Save Time and Resources*
- *Take Total Control of Your Business*

Foreword By

The Plan-As-You-Go Business Plan

Tim Berry

Principal Author of

Business Plan Pro

The Country's Bestselling Business Plan Software

Entrepreneur
Press

Editorial Director: Jere L. Calmes
Cover Design: Desktop Miracles
Production and Composition: Eliot House Productions

This publication is designed to provide accurate and authoritative information in
regard to the subject matter covered. It is sold with the understanding that the publisher is not engaged in rendering legal, accounting or other professional services. If
legal advice or other expert assistance is required, the services of a competent professional person should be sought.

Pushpin with note image ©mmaxer/Shutterstock

Library of Congress Cataloging-in-Publication Data
Berry, Timothy.
The plan-as-you-go business plan/by Tim Berry.
p.   cm.
ISBN-13: 978-1-59918-190-5 (alk. paper)
ISBN-10: 1-59918-190-8
1. Business planning. I. Title.
HD30.28.B4569 2008
658.4'01—dc22   2008015788

Printed in Canada
12 11 10 09 08   10 9 8 7 6 5 4 3 2 1

Contents

Foreword

by Guy Kawasaki

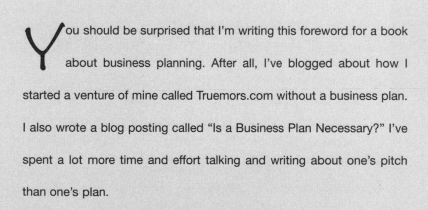

You should be surprised that I'm writing this foreword for a book about business planning. After all, I've blogged about how I started a venture of mine called Truemors.com without a business plan. I also wrote a blog posting called "Is a Business Plan Necessary?" I've spent a lot more time and effort talking and writing about one's pitch than one's plan.

However, it is exactly because of that history that I wanted to write about this book. *Plan-As-You-Go Business Plan* is about planning, not the plan. Tim Berry says that instead of a ponderous document, do the planning that every business needs in order to focus, prioritize, and manage. Do that, and, if that's all you're going to use, do nothing else. Don't sit back waiting for a big plan to be done, get going, start planning, start thinking, and do whatever part that is going to help you run your business better.

In this book, Berry explains how to build your the plan around a core (he calls it the "heart") strategic combination of market, identity, and focus. I like the idea that the real plan is not the output format, but what's supposed to happen, and why, and when, and how much money. It's ideas like this that make me say that everybody running a business should develop a plan, but only in the simple, pragmatic context that this book evangelizes. And that's why you should buy this book.

— Guy Kawasaki, author of
Reality Check and *The Art of the Start*

Preface

Planning is good. You may not need a full formal business plan, but you can certainly use planning to manage. So I've written this book to help you get going quickly, and easily, with only as much planning as you want and need to succeed. That might require a full plan, and it might not.

In an old Peanuts comic strip, Charlie Brown and Lucy are walking on a sidewalk when they see in front of them something that Lucy—who knows everything—identifies as a rare Brazilian butterfly. She starts talking about the wonder of the butterfly having traveled all the way from Brazil, when Charlie Brown looks closer and interrupts: "It's a potato chip."

"Then isn't it even more amazing," Lucy continues, without missing a beat, "that this potato chip got here all the way from Brazil?"

This story reminds me of what's happening to business planning. People who mean to say what I'm saying with this book, that not every business needs a complete formal business plan, end up missing out on planning. And that's a shame.

So I say let's keep it simple and practical. Do as much planning as you'll be able to use. Realize that all plans will change, so think of your plan as ongoing and use it to guide your business. Expect it to change, but use the planning to keep your eyes on the long-term goals even as the details change. It's like planning a trip, for example: having the plan doesn't lock you in, it helps you keep track and revise as needed. Or like dribbling: you keep your eyes on the whole field (or court) while you deal with the ball, watching the play develop without losing track of the goal. Plan as you go.

About This Book

T his is a new approach to business planning. It's *new and different* because it takes what's most important about the traditional business plan idea and applies it better to today's world. And it's a lot *better* than the traditional business plan—quicker, easier, more flexible, more practical, and more useful.

It's been a long time coming. I've been working with business plans for about 30 years now. Startup plans for new companies that didn't yet exist, growth plans, strategic plans, action plans, feasibility plans, lots of plans. One of my startup plans became Borland International, which went public less than four years after it started and made me a lot of money. I did annual plans for Apple Latin America, then Apple Pacific, and then Apple Japan for a combined total of 12 years. I've used business plans to grow my own company to 40 employees and 70 percent market share without outside investment.

Through all these years, I've seen how business planning can be the secret of success for new companies and growing companies. I've seen how the best companies understand planning and regularly develop plans and manage them. Good companies plan.

I've also seen how myths and misunderstandings get in the way. People think—wrongly—that having a plan means getting locked into doing something that doesn't make sense, mindlessly, because it's in the plan. People think—wrongly—that rapid changes make planning less useful, when in fact good planning is one of the best ways to manage change. People think—and this is one of the most damaging misconceptions—that a business plan is hard to do and set in stone with a long list of necessary parts, a ponderous and pompous formal exercise.

The plan-as-you-go business plan is what you need and only what you need. It can be as simple as a 60-second strategy summary that can be delivered in an elevator. For smaller companies it might be that plus a review schedule, milestones table, measurement notes, and a sales forecast. And as companies grow, their plans can grow. Then, when you need the big plan document, you add the additional parts you need and create the document. But you are always planning, and you are never without a plan.

This is not the first business plan book I've done. Unfortunately, I now hate the title of my last business plan book, the most successful, because it sets up exactly the wrong idea: the business

> I've seen how the best companies understand planning and regularly develop plans and manage them.

IMPATIENT? THEN JUMP IN

I understand. Enough of the explanations and positioning; let's get working on a plan. So go ahead, just jump in and do it.

- *Most people like to start with the **heart of the plan**.* Jump to Chapter 3 now, and you'll see what I mean. It's about what really drives your business. Your target market, your business offering, your strategic focus. And don't worry about format; write it, speak it, use bullet points, slides, or whatever.

- *My personal favorite is the **plan review schedule**.* This makes it very clear that you're after planning, and better management, not just a plan. (See page 104.)

- *Another very good starting point is the **sales forecast**.* Some people like to get to the numbers first, and many people do the conceptual thinking while they work the numbers. Your target market, your business offering, your strategic focus are all in your head as you make your sales forecast. That's not a bad way to proceed. (See page 131.)

- *Maybe you want to start with an **expense budget** instead.* Estimate your payroll on an average month. Calculate your burn rate, a very important number, meaning how much money you have to spend per month. (See page 155.)

- *If you're planning to start a business, **startup costs** are a good place to get going.* Make lists of what you need in money, goods, locations, and so forth. (See page 161.)

- *Particularly when you have a team, a **SWOT** (strengths, weaknesses, opportunites, and threats) analysis is a great way to start.* You can jump to the section on SWOT analysis now and begin there. (See page 80.)

- *Some people like to set the scene better, with the **mission statement**, vision, mantra, objectives, or keys to success.* That gives your plan a framework to live in, if you like. (See page 73.)

However, there are some things in business planning, even plan-as-you-go planning, that have to happen in a certain order. For example, you can't really just start with the cash flow statement without having done your sales forecast, burn rate, and some asset and liabilities assumptions.

Still, you can get started fast. I don't blame you. Maybe you'll *jump back here* to continue with the explanations after you've made some progress.

plan as hurdle. The book is titled *Hurdle: The Book on Business Planning*. What's wrong with this is that business planning isn't supposed to be like a hurdle that stands in the way; instead, it's a powerful tool for managing your company better, controlling your business destiny, establishing accountability, and developing teamwork. You should never think of it as a hurdle. It's not an obstacle you overcome; it's a technique that always helps you manage your company better.

So don't stop working. Don't ever let the business plan stand between you and doing business. Get started, get going, and make the plan useful to you from the very first day.

You'll find that strategy in this book. I want you to get started. I expect that you'll be able to do something today that will already be helping your business tomorrow.

TIPS & TRAPS

THE BIG PLAN, ALL AT ONCE

You can also do the big plan all at once! I understand. This new approach is great, but never mind, you need the formal plan. You've been asked for it by somebody who might invest, or a bank loan manager, or a boss. Maybe you're doing it for a business school class. I call these *business plan events*. When you need the old-fashioned full document, so be it; there's a business need, so let's get it done.

We'll get there in this book. You can jump to Chapter 5 right now, and start writing things down, section by section. I'd rather have you develop your *core plan* first, then get the essentials, including the *who, what, when, how much*, the *sales forecast*, and the *burn rate* (the amount of money that flows out of the business each month); but that's up to you. "Get started and get going" means you can also do it the old-fashioned way if you want.

What's Different About This Book?
A Live Book: Web Links

Some things change more often than a book is printed, so I keep the content alive and refreshed on the web. You've got the book as a guide, but let's optimize.

This is the 21st century. I'm not pretending this book lives alone. As I wrote this, I was also working on three blogs myself and contributing to three others as a guest expert. I only recently stopped running a company that lives and breathes web traffic, download sales, conversion rates, page views, visitors, and Google analytics. I was working with Microsoft Office on four computers and on three different office substitutes in the web world, where my documents live online, and I visit them from whichever computer I'm on.

If you're near a computer, go to planasyougo.com.

If you're near a computer, go to planasyougo.com and you'll see what that means for you. It's a new world now; everything changes so quickly. Happily, most of what I have to say will last but there will also be updates, new ideas, tools, and of course new stuff on my blogs and associated websites. Join me there. That's your portal to what else is happening in plan-as-you-go business planning.

I don't expect this book to sit static on the shelf—I expect you to use it. And I don't expect it to sit static as it is—I expect to update it constantly on the web, on my blogs, and as it flows through the world into other books, magazines, software, and so on.

Chapter Updates

Please do check in at planasyougo.com because I will be updating some chapters from time to time. After all, if we're doing plan-as-you-go planning, isn't it also logical that we do write-as-you-go authorship? Things change, not just in your business, but also in the business of business planning.

Information Sources

Resources and references that appear in this book can also change; once again, we're living in the real world here, so we have to deal with change. I'll keep you updated through the planasyougo.com.

The plan-as-you-go business plan isn't big on supporting information that slows down your process, but it is required in some cases, so I've set up the links to update information sources, such as market research pages, industry information, and standard financials, as they become out-of-date.

Software Optional, Not Required

You don't need software to do plan-as-you-go business planning. This book is about the planning—how to do it, why, when, and how to work with the ideas, the people, the problems, the information, the decisions, and, of course, the numbers. It isn't about any particular software.

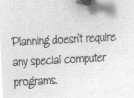

Planning doesn't require any special computer programs.

Planning doesn't require any special computer programs. Plan-as-you-go planning is about results and management, not tools, so you can do it on the back of your hand as far as I'm concerned.

By the way, I am also the principle author of the software Business Plan Pro, published by Palo Alto Software. I'm not going to talk much about that in this book, but I can at least assure you that whatever I'm suggesting you do can be done within that software. And also, look at page 270, there's a deal available.

Quick Action

Jump around. This book is written with that in mind. It's not all sequential. If you want to get going immediately, do so. (I hope you saw the sidebar on page 3.)

I don't expect you to read this book from the first page to the last page. I didn't write it that way and I don't think you'd want to read it that way. This book is about your business, and when you think about your business, your thoughts jump. You go from sales forecast to some new slant on your strategy. One thing reminds you of another.

Please read the chapters in whatever order makes sense to you. I have included cross-references all over the book. Let a thought in one place take you to a different thought in a different place. That's what's supposed to happen.

To help you decide where to go when, I've tried to make the chapter titles and headings maps to the main points in the book.

Jumping Subjects

In his excellent book, *Meatball Sundae* (Portfolio, 2007), Seth Godin points out the growing trend of shorter content, quick jumps of attention, as part of the world we now live in. Instant gratification. Keep it short, like blog posts. You don't want to sit through a long lecture.

Planning isn't sequential.

Business planning is a lot like that, too. You can expect a lot of short subjects. Stories. Sidebars. I want to help you think about your business, what's important, how to do it better. Planning isn't sequential. Thinking comes in short bursts.

The Blogs

From planasyougo.com, you'll find links to other resources: updates, online tools, templates, the proverbial latest and greatest. And I hope you'll also check in and look for what's going on at my regular posting places:

- *Planning, Startups, Stories* (blog.timberry.com). My first blog, sort of a flagship blog. That one gets a lot of my developing work on business planning, plus stories of real companies, including my own, mistakes, occasionally interesting videos, current events, and planning fundamentals.

■ *Up and Running* (upandrunning.entrepreneur.com). My blog on starting a business, hosted at entrepreneur.com. This blog

A WORD ABOUT WORDS

AN APPROACH, NOT A METHOD

The plan-as-you-go business plan is a new approach, a new way of thinking about business planning. It doesn't really change fundamentals, but it does change the focus. It adds some *new angles*, and it's better for you and better for your business.

What's the difference? Why do I make the distinction?

Garr Reynolds, in an introduction to his highly-acclaimed book *Presentation Zen*, says his approach to presentations "is not a method":

Method implies a step-by-step systematic process, something very much planned and linear, with a definite proven procedure that you can pick off a shelf and follow A to Z in a logical orderly fashion.

An approach implies a road, a direction, a frame of mind, perhaps even a philosophy, but not a formula of proven rules to be followed.

I like this distinction. It definitely makes plan-as-you-go planning an approach, not a method. I've spent a lot of years working on step-by-step methods to do business planning. Some of them work. Sometimes. But the whole idea of step-by-step, attractive as it is, reinforces the myth of the business plan as a document or hurdle.

What's the difference? Why does it matter? It's not that important, but I do want to use the idea of an approach instead of a method to emphasize that I don't want this plan-as-you-go concept to become another list of specific steps, or another list of "do it my way" methods. I want this approach, like this book, like your plan, to be yours, not mine. You take what I'm offering here and use what you want from it, in whatever order you want to use it, and make it work for you.

includes examples of actual startups, stories of startups, advice, new ideas, and links to other blogs and outside sources.

■ *I also contribute to some other blogs,* including the Business in General (businessingeneral.com) blog, Small Business Trends (smallbiztrends.com), and the *Huffington Post* (huffing tonpost.com).

Why Plan as You Go?

The plan-as-you-go business plan is better than the standard, old-fashioned, formal business plan for several good reasons.

■ *Everybody in business deserves business planning to help her manage.* That doesn't mean, however, that everybody ought to have a formal plan document written out.

■ *Things change fast.* Planning needs to be quick, flexible, and sensitive to changing assumptions. It's like steering or navigation: eyes up on the horizon, looking at long-term directions, while also managing concrete specifics.

■ *The plan is useless, but planning is essential.* As I wrote this, we were eight years into the 21st century, four years into Web 2.0 and social media, and 30 years into personal computing; it was time to change our views on business planning.

Start with that simple paradox: *the plan is useless, but planning is essential.* That's a quote from former U.S. President Dwight Eisenhower, who had reason to know a lot about planning. He led the Allied forces to victory in Europe during the Second World War.

What's Different About This Approach?

This is a new approach, but some of the principles have been around a long time. Others are just making their debut. Take a look at Chapter 2, on attitude adjustment. The headings there highlight

A WORD ABOUT WORDS

MILITARY QUOTES ON PLANNING

The military relates very well to planning. In business talk about battle plans and war plans, as well as business plans. One of the most recommended books for business is Sun Tzu's *The Art of War*. I use Eisenhower's quote "The plan is useless, but planning is essential" frequently, in writing, speaking, and teaching about planning. He makes a critical point.

There's also the famous line: "No battle plan ever survives the first encounter with the enemy," often attributed to Colin Powell, but also to Field Marshall Helmuth Carl Bernard von Moltke.

the differences between this approach and the standard planning method. If you're impatient, consider this quick summary:

- *It's about planning, not just a plan.* If you don't review your plan regularly, you're wasting your time. The review schedule is absolutely essential.
- *It's about appropriately-sized planning.* Start simple, maybe with your core strategy, sales forecast, and milestones table, for example. Maybe that's all you're really going to use at the beginning. If so, then that's all you should do. Grow it as you need to. Use it at every step. Form follows function.
- *It separates the plan from its output.* You can have a plan without having a formal complete business plan document. The plan is what's going to happen. The output might be a document, speech, presentation, or something else.
- *It separates the supporting information from the plan.* Not everybody needs to develop market forecasts and management team profiles to convince an outsider to invest. Most people know their market and want to plan their business, and they

manage it without spending a lot of time proving that the market exists.

Why Is This Approach Better?

The plan-as-you-go business plan has several important advantages over the old-fashioned, formal business plan document, often seen as hurdle. For example:

- *It gets results*. It helps you manage your business. It optimizes your efforts. You start simply with what you need and only what you need, and you grow your plan as you grow your company. When there's a need for more—like more formalized descriptions for outsiders, or proof of concept or market for outsiders, or description of the management team for outsiders, then you create it.
- *It's faster and easier*. Call it right-size business planning. Start anywhere, get going. Maybe in the beginning it's just a sales forecast or an expense budget; maybe it's the sense of core strategy. You do what you need first and grow it organically.
- *It manages change better than the normal business plan*. This pulls assumptions to the top, where they are visible. It recognizes that change is constant. It focuses on the management process that absorbs change without losing the proactive management that takes change to heart.
- *It's more realistic*. Today's world requires flexible planning that builds on actual needs and uses, rather than a recipe or list of components.
- *It's within your ability and grasp*. You don't need a consultant. It's a matter of laying down the basics, like tracks, and then following them. It doesn't have to be big, it doesn't have to be formally written, it doesn't have to have a specific list of components or recipe. It's about what works.

■ *It's just plain the right way to do it.* I'm sorry, I know that seems arrogant, but I've been in the business of business planning for 30 years now. I've seen successes and failures, and I've seen what works.

Chapter Outline

I don't expect you to read from start to finish. I wouldn't. So here's a guide to where you might want to go. The book is divided into six chapters. Following is an outline of the contents of each chapter.

Chapter	Title	Description
1	About This Book	You're here now. Describes what's in this book for you, how to use it, what's new and different about my approach, and why would you want a plan-as-you-go business plan anyhow.
2	Attitude Adjustment	This book is not about your traditional formal business plan. The plan grows organically. It's a new way of doing it. Look for information on how to start, on form and function, on accountability and mapping, and in general on a new way of thinking about business planning. The plan isn't a document and it isn't anything more than what you'll use today to make your business better. You don't have to complete a checklist. However, you do want to use planning to manage your business better. Do what you have to do to leave tracks you can follow up on.
3	The Heart of the Plan	The heart of the plan is your core strategy. It's an interrelated combination of business identity, target market, business offering, and strategic focus. It can be written out, or not.

Chapter	Title	Description
4	Flesh and Bones	This chapter is about what's going to happen, when. Who's going to do it? How much will it cost? The first of three parts includes the action plan with milestones, tasks, and responsibilities. The second is about basic numbers, which include the sales forecast, expense budget, maybe the startup costs (if and only if you're a startup). The third is about about cash-flow traps.
5	Dressing and Growing	Here's where I fill out the rest of the plan and bring it up to the full document that you'll need if you have what I call a business plan event, meaning you have to show a plan to outsiders. I give you the full financial forecast in detail, plus what you need for supporting information, and how to present that as an elevator speech, summary, pitch presentation, or full-blown, complete formal business plan document.
6	Planning Process	This is about making your plan-as-you-go planning into a vital management process that will help you achieve your goals and build your business better. Chapter 6 covers the process of review and revision as well as managing the plan.

Read This Even If You Read Nothing Else

This book, my work, plan-as-you-go planning is about making your business planning a powerful process that helps you determine your business's future, guide your business to the future you want for it, set strategy, manage, and implement. Your planning should be a very powerful tool for driving your business. That includes steering. Keeping the long term visible while minding the details in the short term.

The essence of the plan is its heart, its flesh, and its bone. It isn't necessarily a document, or a presentation, or a speech, or a summary; it's what you're doing and what's supposed to happen. The output of that might vary. Its actual physical existence might be as simple as thoughts in your head, at the beginning, and—I really hope—will quickly become a collection of words and pictures and numbers you keep on your computer.

The Heart of the Plan: The Core Strategy

1. *Who you are*. As a company, if you are one, or as an individual if you're just starting a one-person business. *It's your identity*. Your DNA. Especially what you do well, differently, better; long-term objectives. Goals. Dreams. What do you like to do? Keep the focus in mind, too; that is, think about who you aren't, what you don't do well.

2. *Whom you reach*. That's a customer, a company that buys from you, a client, a beneficiary. Your target market. By the way, it's hard to pull this apart from how they find you, how they know who you are and what you do. Keep focus in mind: who is your target, and what's different about your target that narrows the focus better. Whom don't you reach on purpose? How is your target different from the rest?

3. *What you do for your target*. Fill a need, perform a service, offer a benefit. *What business are you in?* Think of focus as well, meaning what you don't do for your customer.

You can probably see here why I might call these items *identity*, *market*, and *offering*—more standard terms, that sound more MBA-like. Also, I might call them the *tricameral heart* of the plan.

Is this strategy? Maybe, when done well. Strategy is focus. Make that heart of your plan strategic by focusing more narrowly on the most important elements. Narrow your sense of identity to focus on core competencies, what

Strategy is focus.

LIKE DRIBBLING

Think of soccer or basketball. You get control of the ball near your own goal (or basket), and you want to dribble it forward to the opponent's goal. Ideally you have a plan. You're going to pass it up the side, and from there a play will develop. Or some other plan.

And things change rapidly. The opposing players surprise you by doing something different from what you expected.

You watch the play developing. You keep your eyes up to see the field (or the court), but you also focus on the ball and the details of dribbling, probably at the same time.

This is a good example of planning as you go. You watch the field and the details at the same time. You expect things to change. You expect to react to the change quickly.

So it's not that you don't have a plan, or that you don't want planning. It's that you want planning to be very fast and flexible and adaptive. The goals remain the same, but the detailed plan changes.

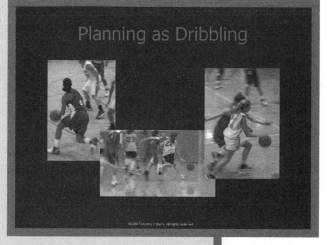

Planning as Dribbling

really makes you different. Concentration is power. Narrow your market to a finely cut target segment, the people and companies who really need you and want you—those who really get it. Narrow your offering to set yourself apart, differentiate, position yourself well. It's what you're not doing and why not. Focus on your business's unique keys to success. Resist the temptation to please everybody, do everything, offer it all.

The Flesh and Bones

1. *Assumptions*. Always list your assumptions, and keep that list at the front of your plan. Things are always changing. Listing your assumptions helps you remember to review them frequently.

2. *Review schedule*. It's essential. No way around it. Please don't do a plan without scheduling times to review the plan and share results with participants and make corrections. At Palo Alto Software, we did it on the third Thursday of every month, for years. "We" were the people who ran the company, three or four of us in the early years, five or ten later on. Every quarter you should dig into the strategy. And you need to set those schedules for review ahead of time, so everybody knows and can plan accordingly. This is where managers are going to track progress against goals, share with peers, and coordinate. Review milestones, review results, review changing assumptions.

3. *Metrics*. It starts with money. Sales. Costs. Expenses. Taxes, interest, profits. Assets, liabilities, capital. That boils down to money in the bank, cash flow. But be creative, beyond money: think about drivers, and nonmonetary metrics like customers, deliveries, complaints, calls, presentations, trips, meals, people served, client companies, repeat business, whatever. Everybody needs metrics. You want to be able to track progress, remember?

4. *Who does what?* Call it management team, management structure, organization—it boils down to who does what. Who's in charge? Who's responsible for what metrics?

5. *When?* Who does what when? Milestones. Dates and deadlines. Concrete specifics.

6. *How much will that cost?* Who does what when; how much will it cost; and how much will it generate? Budgets. Forecasts. Tie

down the concrete specifics related to business activities, tasks, managers. Your plan should leave tracks.

15 REASONS YOU NEED A BUSINESS PLAN

Why do you want a business plan? You already know the obvious reasons, but there are so many other good reasons to create a business plan that many business owners don't know about. So, just for a change, let's take a look at a longer-than-usual list of the most important reasons you need a business plan.

1. *Grow your existing business.* Establish strategy and allocate resources according to strategic priority. You can find more information about growing your business with a business plan by reading my article "Existing Companies Need Planning, Too," at bplans.com.

2. *Create a new business.* Use a plan to establish the right steps to starting a new business, including what you need to do, what resources will be required, and what you expect to happen.

3. *Set specific objectives for managers.* Good management requires setting specific objectives and then tracking and following up. I'm surprised how many existing businesses manage without a plan. How do they establish what's supposed to happen? In truth, most of the people who think they don't plan are really just taking a shortcut and planning in their head—and good for them if they can do it—but as your business grows, you want to organize and plan better and communicate the priorities better. Be strategic. Develop a plan; don't just wing it.

4. *Deal with displacement.* Displacement is probably by far the most important practical business concept you've never heard of. It goes like this: "Whatever you do rules out something else you don't do." Displacement lives at the heart of all small-business strategy. And most people have never heard of it.

5. *Share and explain business objectives with your management team, employees, and new hires.* Make selected portions of your business plan part of your new employee training.

15 REASONS YOU NEED A BUSINESS PLAN, CONTINUED

6. *Share your strategy, priorities and specific action points with your spouse, partner, or significant other.* Your business life goes by so quickly: a rush of answering phone calls, putting out fires, and so on. Don't the people in your personal life need to know what's supposed to be happening? Don't you want them to know?

7. *Hire new people.* This is another new obligation (a fixed cost) that increases your risk. How will new people help your business grow and prosper? What exactly are they supposed to be doing? The rationale for hiring should be in your business plan.

8. *Decide whether or not to rent new space.* Rent is a new obligation, usually a fixed cost. Do your growth prospects and plans justify taking on this increased fixed cost? Shouldn't that be in your business plan?

9. *Seek investment for a business, whether it's a startup or not.* Investors need to see a business plan before they decide whether or not to invest. They'll expect the plan to cover all the main points.

10. *Back up a business loan application.* Like investors, lenders want to see the plan and will expect the plan to cover the main points.

11. *Develop new business alliances.* Use your plan to set targets for new alliances, and use selected portions of your plan to communicate with partners.

12. *Decide whether you need new assets, how many, and whether to buy or lease them.* Use your business plan to help decide what's going to happen in the long term, which should be an important input to the classic make vs. buy decision. How long will this important purchase last in your plan?

13. *Deal with professionals.* Share selected highlights or your plans with your attorneys and accountants, and, if this is relevant to you, consultants.

14. *Sell your business.* Usually the business plan is a very important part of selling the business. Help buyers understand what you have, what it's worth, and why they want it.

---

15 REASONS YOU NEED A BUSINESS PLAN, CONTINUED

15. *Perform a valuation of the business for formal transactions related to divorce, inheritance, estate planning, or tax issues.* Valuation is the term for establishing how much your business is worth. Usually that takes a business plan, as well as a professional with experience. The plan tells the valuation expert what your business is doing, when, and why as well as how much that will cost and how much it will produce.

Adapted from a column for entrepreneur.com.

The Rest: Dressing It Up

Separate the plan from the dressing. The plan is what, why, how, who, and how much. Dressing is supporting information.

This is important: form follows function. So of course you want a plan, no matter who you are or how big or how new your company is. However, that doesn't mean that everybody needs to have the full formal business plan with all the supporting information.

For example, you might be running or growing or starting your own one-person business. You feel very comfortable about knowing your customers and your market and you've got a strategy. Why are you writing all this down, formalizing it, making a big project that you don't really need? No good reason. Planning is about the decisions it causes; it's not about showing off your knowledge.

This is important: form follows function.

Example: You're starting a new coffee-roasting business in Bend, Oregon. It's just you and your spouse and a close family member who is also investing. You want to develop your strategy and cash-flow projections and decide who will do what, and you want to track progress against goals, so you do need a plan. But it's not going to be a formal business plan document with a heavy market analysis and competitive analysis. It's going to stay on your computer. You may or may not do a special research and analysis project for this plan, but either way, you're comfortable with your sense of the market and the strategy you're developing.

So if you don't have to do the formal plan, because you're not required to by the investor or the bank, then don't. And when you do want to do the plan, because things are changing (maybe you're entering a contest, or looking for an investor, or the bank asks for it), then you take the next step of developing the document with all the supporting information.

You do what the business needs demand—no more, no less.

Do You Have a Business Plan Event?

Danger: Don't confuse not having a business plan event with not needing or wanting a business plan.

The business plan event forces you to present a plan. It might be that you're seeking outside investment, or applying for business financing from a bank or other lender, or you're involved in a business class that requires a business plan, or you're going to enter a venture contest that requires a business plan.

The business plan event forces you to present a plan.

It's because of these business plan events that people confuse the idea of *needing* a business plan with wanting business planning. Suddenly experts can make themselves feel good by advising people not to do the formal business plan because they don't have a business plan event. It sounds like they are saying *don't plan*, when what they mean is more like *don't bother to do the big, ponderous formal plan document*.

This potential confusion is dangerous. Don't deprive yourself of planning just because you don't have to present a formal plan to outsiders. Plan your business regardless. That's why I'm suggesting that you plan as you go.

About that Big Plan

There is a lot to be said for the formal business plan. Concretely, it covers all the bases. You get a full review of a business, soup to nuts, as they say, and if you follow one of the standard outlines, you're less likely to leave something out. That makes things conceptually easier.

So while I'm not recommending that big formal plan for all, you certainly can start with the plan-as-you-go plan and end up with the formal business plan. And I'd hate for this book not to tell you how.

Allow me, then, to go over the standard contents of the standard plan and relate them to parts of this book. I'll give you the jumps, so to speak.

Sequence of Components in a Standard Business Plan	What It Is and Where to Read More About It
1.0 Executive Summary 1.1 Objectives 1.2 Mission (or mantra) 1.3 Keys to Success	These are good things to think about. You can jump there now if you want, specifically to my discussion on missions and mantras, objectives, and keys to success. These are in Chapter 3, "The Heart of the Plan."
2.0 Company Summary 2.1 Company Ownership 2.2 Company History (for ongoing companies) or Startup Plan (for new companies) 2.3 Company Locations and Facilities	You're not going to do this until you have to. It's dressing (see Chapter 5), something you'll do when you need to describe your plan to outsiders.

Sequence of Components in a Standard Business Plan	What It Is and Where to Read More About It
3.0 Products and Services 3.1 Product and Service Description 3.2 Competitive Comparison 3.3 Sales Literature 3.4 Sourcing 3.5 Technology 3.6 Future Products and Services	You do a lot of core thinking about what your business offering is, and why people want to buy from you when you work on the heart of the plan (see Chapter 3). But don't necessarily write out all of these descriptions unless you need a full plan document, which is discussed in Chapter 5.

4.0 Market Analysis Summary
4.1 Market Segmentation
4.2 Target Market Segment Strategy
    4.2.1 Market Needs
    4.2.2 Market Trends
    4.2.3 Market Growth
4.3 Industry Analysis
    4.3.1 Industry Participants
    4.3.2 Distribution Patterns
    4.3.3 Competition and Buying Patterns
    4.3.4 Main Competitors
	Your sense of who your target customer is, what you're selling him, why he buys, and what business you're in is all in Chapter 3, "The Heart of the Plan."
	
	However, the plan-as-you-go plan separates the market analysis that influences strategy and the market analysis that proves market potential for outsiders from the main plan. It's covered in Chapter 5, "Dressing and Growing." Unless it drives your decisions, leave it for later.

5.0 Strategy and Implementation Summary
    5.1 Strategy Pyramids
    5.2 Value Proposition
    5.3 Competitive Edge
    5.4 Marketing Strategy
        5.4.1 Positioning Statements
        5.4.2 Pricing Strategy
        5.4.3 Promotion Strategy
	Your strategy is discussed in Chapter 3, "The Heart of the Plan." Writing it out and dressing it up is explained in Chapter 5, "Dressing and Growing."
	
	The sales forecast is discussed in Chapter 4, "Flesh and Bones." So is the milestones table. Milestones are critical to the action plan and the sales forecast is the key to the financial plan (see Chapter 4).

Sequence of Components in a Standard Business Plan	What It Is and Where to Read More About It

5.4.4 Distribution Patterns
5.4.5 Marketing Programs
5.5 Sales Strategy
   5.5.1 Sales Forecast
   5.5.2 Sales Programs
5.6 Strategic Alliances
5.7 Milestones
	Implementation and plan vs. actual analysis comes up again in Chapter 6, on the planning process and planning as management.

6.0 Management Summary 6.1 Organizational Structure 6.2 Management Team 6.3 Management Team Gaps 6.4 Personnel Plan	Your personnel budget is covered in Chapter 4, "The Flesh and Bones." The rest of this is description for outsiders, covered in Chapter 5, "Dressing and Growing."
7.0 Financial Plan 7.1 Important Assumptions 7.2 Key Financial Indicators 7.3 Break-Even Analysis 7.4 Projected Profit and Loss 7.5 Projected Cash Flow 7.6 Projected Balance Sheet 7.7 Business Ratios 7.8 Long-Term Plan	I discuss assumptions, sales forecast, expense forecast, and some cash-flow traps in Chapter 4. You really can't be planning without them. Then, in Chapter 5, we go from there to the full financial plan, including the standard projections you'll need to create a complete financial picture for outsiders.

CHAPTER

2

Attitude Adjustment

The plan-as-you-go business plan is not your formal, traditional business plan. You don't fill in a checklist or cover all the bases as defined by some recipe somewhere. It's about planning and running a business in the real world, in this millennium, whether you are going to show some big plan document to somebody else or not. This chapter covers the attitude adjustment involved in this new approach to planning. The following table outlines the main sections of this chapter.

Item	Description
Start Anywhere. Get Going.	Start with concepts, start with numbers, start with whatever suits you. It doesn't matter. Do something today that you can use tomorrow.
Form Follows Function	Your plan is not necessarily a document. It's what's going to happen. Think it, speak it, write it out simply in bullets, or use pictures. No extra struggle. Use what you need.
Let It Evolve Organically, as You Need It To	Do what you can use now, then use it, and then you can grow it over time as you need to. When a business plan event happens and you need to show it to somebody outside your company, then you add to it and make it more formal.
Fundamental Management	It's not just a plan, it's your business. You should use the planning process to manage better, achieve your goals, and work proactively instead of reactively.
Mixing Numbers and Words: Keep It Simple	Use only what you need.
Inside Out from the Heart	A good plan is like an artichoke, with the core strategy in the middle and the rest of the plan—what's going to happen, when, how, and so on—surrounding it.
Separate Supporting Information from the Plan	One of the big wins with the plan-as-you-go business plan is that if you aren't going to use the complete market analysis, industry analysis, and the rest of the supporting information, you don't formally develop them.
Planning, Not Accounting	Although your business plan projections look a lot like accounting statements, they aren't. Where accounting goes into minute detail, planning needs summary and aggregation. They are educated guesses, not tax reports. You should approach them with flexibility and an understanding of how much uncertainty is involved.

Item	Description
It Has to Be Your Plan	You don't need just a business plan, written by anybody. You need to know your own plan, inside and out, with all the details. The core should be your own thinking. Use consultants wisely or not at all.
Control Your Destiny	One of the most important wins you get from good planning is controlling your own destiny in business. You set your future goals and steps to achieve them. While people think you have to have a plan to show somebody else, you want a plan as a tool to manage your own business future.

Start Anywhere. Get Going.

Think of your business plan as a set of blocks, like interrelated pieces. You don't have to have the whole block structure done before you take any next steps. Start your blocks where you like. Some common blocks are the mantra (page 73), the sales forecast (page 131), the mission statement (78), the keys to success (79), maybe a SWOT analysis (page 80), and the heart of your plan (Chapter 3), as in the whole discussion of *who* needs your product or service and *why* and *what* it is. A sales forecast is a block, and so is an employee or personnel plan, as in laying out month by month how many people will be working in your company and how much each of them will be paid.

The key here is that you don't get bogged down on having a finished business plan before you do anything

© Leva Geneviciene/iStock photo

else. You're planning as you go. You've heard the stories of people who spent months developing their plan but never got started. So instead of that, think of the blocks. Choose where you want to start. Get going.

Start Wherever You Like

The blocks idea also saves you from the tyranny of sequence. You don't have to start at the beginning and work through to the end. You can jump in and start wherever you want.

- *Mission statement, maybe?* Define for yourself what your company will do for its customers, for its employees, and for its owners. Mission statements are a bit last century, perhaps doomed forever to Dilbert-related derision, but that's still where some people start.
- *Maybe you're a numbers person.* That's OK, don't apologize— business planning needs that, too. I was a literature major in college but I still like to start my business planning with a sales forecast. Then I'll do some conceptual work, then go back to costs and expenses, classic budgeting work, then back to basics.
- *Business plans have hearts, like artichokes do.* In both, their hearts are their core, the best part. I thought of this analogy when somebody I know and respect suggested that the heart of a business plan is the marketing plan, meaning its identity, positioning, differentiation, the sense of what business you're in and why people will buy from you. That's a great place to start.
- *Some plans start with a product or prototype product.* Maybe your first block is a bill of materials for manufacturing the new thing. That's OK too; that's a block, you can jump in there.
- *There are lots more blocks.* The mantra. The vision. A market analysis. A market forecast. Personnel strategy. Financial strategy. Some people like to build an equity plan first, focusing on

TIPS & TRAPS

FILTER IDEAS FROM OPPORTUNITIES

Business ideas are interesting, exciting stuff to build a business by, but they are worth nothing (in general) until somebody builds a company around them.

Opportunities are the best of the ideas. An idea is just that. An opportunity is an idea you can implement. You have the resources and know-how to do it. There is a market. You can make money on it, and the investment will be worth it.

© Méhmet Dilsiz/iStock photo

Good business planning filters the opportunities from the ideas. Apply the planning process to the idea to make it an opportunity. Determine the market strength, what exactly is needed, how long it will take, how much money it will take, what people are required. Lay it out into steps.

Not all ideas can survive the rigor of planning. Some fall by the wayside, ending up as interesting ideas that aren't really opportunities.

Some of the factors that count:

- *Risk vs. return.* Is what it takes to pursue this idea worth the likely return? This is not scientific. It depends a lot on your business's attitude about risk and what other opportunities are available.

- *Realism.* How realistic are the forecasts? Give them a good look. Are you pushing the forecast to make things work?

- *Resources.* What will really be required? Think of people, know-how, skills, compensation, implied risk (paying people to build this company up). What are the startup costs, including expenses required and assets required?

- *Market potential.* The heart of your sales forecast is the market potential. How much do people want or need the business offering?

- *Business potential.* How much money can the business make? How will this impact the business? How big is this opportunity, overall?

how many shares exist, how many the founders get, and how many the investors get.

Don't Worry About Finishing

A good business plan is never done. It's the launch of a planning process, and you want to understand from the very beginning that if you ever think your plan is done, your business is probably finished. You'll have to review and revise regularly to keep your business going. Assumptions will change, your forecasts will be wrong, and the art of management will be figuring out when to revise the plan to accommodate changing reality, and when to stick to the parts of the plan that will work if you hold your course. That's a paradox, of course, and that's why we (owners and managers) do it instead of computers.

Form Follows Function

Your plan-as-you-go business plan is no more than what you need to run your business. In the beginning, it might be as simple as an elevator speech, as explained in Chapter 5. Be able to talk through those key points: the customer story, what makes you unique, how you're focusing and on what you're focusing, and, if it comes to that, your close—what you want from whoever is listening.

Or it might be a simple sales forecast and, perhaps, a burn rate in the very beginning because you know what you're doing—maybe you've been doing it for years already and you don't need to verbalize it right at this moment—and you'll set those figures down and start tracking them.

Planning comes in many forms. Think of it as analogous to motion in athletics. In

Builds Function, Not Form

© Cyril LeRoux/iStock photo

TRUE STORY

A MILITARY EXERCISE

In Chapter 4 of his book *Blink*, Malcolm Gladwell describes how Paul Van Riper, a retired Marine commander, drove the U.S. military to fits in a war exercise called Millennium Challenge. It's a brilliant argument for the plan-as-you-go approach compared with the traditional plan method.

The Millennium Challenge was an exercise designed to test the military's ability to deal with a simulated war in the Middle East. It pitted a very large team (Blue Team) equipped with a very detailed battle plan, and a lot of computer models and simulations, against a very small team (Red Team) led by Van Riper, experienced, self confident, and good at making quick decisions.

"Blue Team had their databases and matrixes and methodologies for systematically understanding the intentions of the enemy. Red Team was commanded by a man who looked at a long-haired, unkempt, seat-of-the-pants commodities trader yelling and pushing and making a thousand instant decisions an hour and saw in him a soul mate."

As you've probably already guessed, Blue Team is the might of the military, and Red Team is essentially one smart guy who starts with a plan and revises it constantly as the battle ensues.

When the game was actually played, Van Riper surprised the blue team quickly with a move not in its plans, and as they reacted to that, he surprised them again, and quickly caused considerable unexpected damage to a much larger force. It was all simulated and hypothetical, but the result was that the quick-to-react team with flexible planning beat the pants off the very detailed plan team that couldn't react to changes.

"Had Millennium Challenge been a real war instead of just an exercise, 20,000 American servicemen and women would have been killed before their own army had even fired a shot."

That was pretty hard for the military to explain. They analyzed it a lot.

"There were numerous explanations from the analysts at JFCOM (Joint Forces Command Center) about exactly what happened that day in July. Some would say that it was an artifact of the

TRUE STORY

A MILITARY EXERCISE, CONTINUED

particular way war games are run. Others would say that in real life, the ships would never have been as vulnerable as they were in the game. But none of the explanations changes the fact that Blue Team suffered a catastrophic failure. The rogue commander did what rogue commanders do. He fought back, yet somehow this fact caught Blue Team by surprise."

Implicitly, the problem was that the big team full of computers and data trusted a static plan, while the other team didn't.

Red Team's powers of rapid cognition were intact, and Blue Team's were not.

So relate that to the planning we want: planning that responds to rapidly changing reality. Not just "Duh, I can't plan, I don't know the future," and not just "Why plan? Why bother," and not "We have to follow the plan," but planning as you go.

so many different sports, the winners practice economy of motion, repeated muscle memory. Another way to look at it: in design and mechanics, the fewer moving parts, the better. If you have to squint conceptually to see the key points, squint down on the elements you'll be able to track and then revisit.

It's not about the text, or the form of the thing, until that becomes related to the function. When you're doing a business plan as part of a graduate business school class, then yes, it has to be complete and look good and read well; editing and format matter. When you're doing a plan for an investment group that is going to pass it around among the partners, then it matters. But you don't want to get bogged down in format when it's just you and your spouse and you simply want to think through what's required.

So the plan is a collection of concepts in the middle, surrounded by specifics that have to be done. Around the core you put a collection of metrics (page 107) to be measured and tracked (lots of them are sales, expenses, and the like, but not all), task assignments and responsibilities for different people, dates and deadlines, budgets, and so on. That's your plan.

From that core plan, you spin off various outputs (see Figure 2.1). You take the highest highlights of the plan and 60 seconds or so to

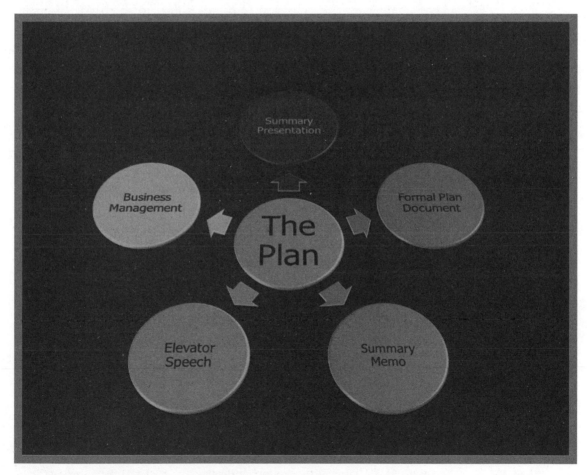

Figure 2.1 **Possible Outputs from Your Plan**

explain it in an elevator speech. That's one output. Or you write it all out carefully, and add supporting information about the market and the industry and the backgrounds of the management team, and it's a plan document. Or you create a 20-minute, 10-slide summary with PowerPoint or Keynote slides, and that's a pitch presentation for potential investors. Or you create a cover letter or cover e-mail, about a page or so, along with a five- to ten-page written summary, and that's a summary memo. Or you do none of these; you simply keep that plan as a collection of bullet points, of pictures, financial projections, and a list of things to be done by whom and when and for how much money, and share it with your team. In that last case you don't ever edit or polish it, or sweat the page headers and page footers or font size. You just use it to manage your company.

Notice that none of these outputs stands as something you do instead of the plan. And none of these outputs is really the plan. The plan exists at the core, and you create the outputs as needed.

With all of these various iterations and outputs, always keep assumptions on top, where you can see them for every review meeting. Minding the changing assumptions is one of the significant advantages of the plan-as-you-go approach over the more traditional methods.

I ran a business for years during which the plan was shared only between me and my wife, mostly, enhanced by sales forecasts and burn rate. During those formative years there was no need for anything else. When it was time for an elevator speech, either one of us could do it. When there was need for a written business plan—it came up first when we set up a merchant account to be able to accept credit cards, in 1988—then we settled down for a while and wrote it out as it was, conceptually, at that time. We always knew what we wanted to do, but we also knew our key assumptions, and we tracked them as they changed, and revised the plan. A lot of that was verbal, between two people.

The plan exists at the core, and you create the outputs as needed.

MYTH BUSTER

IT'S NOT ONE SIZE FITS ALL

It's amazing how long business experts, teachers, coaches, and advisors have swallowed and even spread the idea that a business plan is some sort of standard document, a predictable standard task with a generally accepted set of parameters to define it.

It just isn't so. Like so many other things in business, the business planning should be appropriate to the needs of the business.

Just about every business needs to build and understand its heart, that core element of strategy that's about what you're doing for whom, who you are and what you want to do.

Beyond that, every business ought to be able to set down some tracks it can then follow and manage, watching progress toward goals. The sales forecast is the most obvious set of tracks. Milestones, like who does what, when, and for how much, are almost always useful. And don't forget the burn rate.

And as your company grows, you can grow your plan and your planning. Grow it like an artichoke grows, with leaves—more details, more specifics, more description—surrounding the heart.

What's important is that you do the planning you need to run your business better. Not the one-size-fits-all plan, but the just-big-enough plan to give you better direction and management without wasting any time or effort on documentation you won't use.

As the business grew, the verbal plan with the forecast stopped working. Things became more complicated. Employees needed to know about the plan and join in its formation and then its implementation. So we moved it into bullet points on the computer and tied those to forecasts, and began tracking in a group, in more detail.

We then began to do annual plans more formally, writing out chapters, and conducting review meetings every month. With each annual plan we'd go out and take a new, fresh look at the market.

We had people doing nothing but marketing, and they developed segmentations and forecasts and supporting information. It was part of their job.

Are you recognizing yourself somewhere along this line?

Eventually we wanted to bring in outside investment. That was during the dotcom boom when valuations were very high, so we thought it would be a good time to lock in the value with some cash out. We produced very formal plans every three months during that period.

The speech isn't instead of the plan, and the pitch isn't instead of the plan, but that doesn't mean you don't plan if nobody outside your company is going to read about it. Your plan should always be there as the source of these outputs, so you're ready to produce them when you need to.

Let It Evolve Organically, as You Need It To

You see in lots of places (including later in this book, in Chapter 5) recommended outlines for business plans. With the plan-as-you-go plan, in contrast to the more weighty and ominous outlines, you're probably going to start simple. For example, see the outline in Figure 2.2.

You could jump right now to Chapter 3 to see what I mean by the core strategy, or to Chapter 4 for details about the action plan and the financial plan. If you don't jump, then just take my word for it: these can be very simple pieces. I do recommend that you write them down or record them somehow, but keep it simple. Bullet points are probably enough, maybe some pictures for slides, or even just an elevator speech.

As your business planning evolves, you'll add pieces to fit your needs. Eventually, when you have a business plan event, you may find it useful to fill in a lot of information intended mainly for outsiders, such as the market analysis, industry analysis, detailed financial analysis, and descriptions of the company, the management team, and so on. But don't think you don't have a plan just because you start simply, with what you really need.

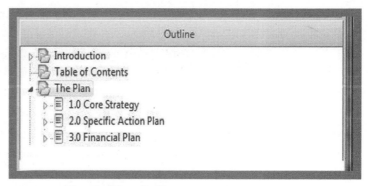

Figure 2.2 **Simple Plan Outline**

Fundamental Management

Planning should become management and better business, long-term progress toward goals, prioritizing, and focus, but you have to do it. It's up to you to make your planning work. It's not really

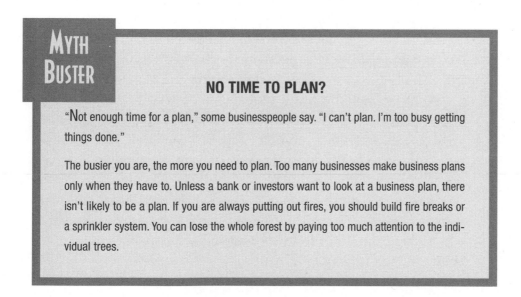

NO TIME TO PLAN?

"Not enough time for a plan," some businesspeople say. "I can't plan. I'm too busy getting things done."

The busier you are, the more you need to plan. Too many businesses make business plans only when they have to. Unless a bank or investors want to look at a business plan, there isn't likely to be a plan. If you are always putting out fires, you should build fire breaks or a sprinkler system. You can lose the whole forest by paying too much attention to the individual trees.

about the plan, per se; it's about the discipline to use the plan to run the business.

If you think I am pushing too hard on this, feel free to jump into the planning at any time by skipping ahead to another chapter.

The plan-as-you-go business plan normally grows organically; it evolves as your business evolves. With monthly review schedules and performance tracking, your planning, unlike the classic plan document, stays alive and present—on top of your mind, where you consider it regularly.

For that to work, you have to keep assumptions at the forefront. You have to develop accountability by setting goals, usually with metrics, and then following up on performance with people.

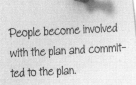

People become involved with the plan and committed to the plan.

Keep the plan visible, to all team members, using the review meetings if nothing else. Ideally, key points, numbers, metrics, and assumptions will be somewhere that team members can see them.

People become involved with the plan and committed to the plan. You can't really have people believing in the planning goals if they don't participate. Goals have to be credible and realistic. People who are charged with implementing the plan need to be involved in developing and managing the plan.

What we have here is a problem somewhat like healthy diet and regular exercise. Pretty much everybody agrees that those are good things, but not everybody actually eats well and exercises regularly. So too with good planning process. Knowing what to do doesn't mean you'll do it.

Hint: Set the review schedule ahead of time and invite the team members. Show the metrics. Suggest some key agenda points that you garner from the milestones. People need to believe in accountability for accountability to work.

I talk about this more in Chapter 6, "Planning Process."

Mixing Numbers and Words: Keep It Simple

Lots of people think of themselves as either word (or concept) people or numbers people. In business planning, however, it's hard to separate the two. Even the words and concepts people need numbers—the sales forecast, the expense budget, other metrics—to make their planning real. And the numbers people need to move away from the numbers for long enough to think through the core strategy: how their company is different, what their customers want from them, and how to deliver it.

The problems come when people get bogged down. Some people fear writing; they think of the empty page, spelling errors, grammar errors, bad days in school. Some people fear math. They think of arithmetic errors, red marks on papers, not being qualified.

And the magic solution is just keeping it simple.

■ As for words and concepts, particularly at the beginning, think of the core as that elevator speech, maybe a few bullet points, but not a term paper or well-written prose. It doesn't matter. Nobody but you is reading it. You can dress it up later when you actually need to show it to an outsider.

■ For the numbers, start with just a few basics. Do a sales forecast. Do an expense budget. Be mindful of the cash-flow traps, watch your cash balance, but don't think you need a full financial forecast from day one. Just create some estimates you can track and review and manage by comparing plan vs. actual. If and only if you're a startup, do your starting costs, too.

You may have a business plan event, in which case you'll probably want to do the full explanations with supporting information, covering the bigger market picture, team background, company history, and a complete financial forecast including sales, personnel, profit

The problems come when people get bogged down.

and loss statement, balance sheet, cash flow, even the business ratios, and probably a break-even analysis. You may also include what you're going to do with the money you're seeking, how much of your company you're trading for investment, and so on.

And for the words and concepts people, you already have somebody running the numbers of your company. You have to have that to survive administration and taxes. If you're just starting, then you can usually find somebody who understands basic business numbers so you can add those skills to your team. Remember, it doesn't have to be just you; you can build a team with co-founders or partners or contractors or employees. Somebody will have to run the numbers once you get going.

If you're a number person, I think I know you pretty well even though I was a lit major in college and wrote for a living for years. I discovered numbers in business later, when I got the MBA. You are probably keeping the main concepts in your head—things like positioning, differentiation, strategy, and focus—because you think about them through the numbers. Don't sweat the format or the mistakes or the sentence structure; just tell your story. And start with the numbers; that works just as well.

Remember, with the plan-as-you-go business plan, the idea is to start anywhere and get going. Build it as you need it.

That having been said, I want to share a words-and-numbers-together story. This is from my book *Hurdle: The Book on Business Planning*:

> In 1974, I switched from general journalism, writing for *United Press International* from Mexico City, to business journalism, writing for *Business International* and *McGraw-Hill World News*. With the switch, I found myself covering business and economics instead of general news, writing for (among others) *BusinessWeek* and *Business Latin America*. Because I thought it would be nice to have some idea what I was writing

about, I went to the local graduate school at night for courses in general economics, accounting, finance, and marketing.

As I learned about macroeconomics and how to read financial statements, I discovered that the truth in business is almost always a combination of words and numbers, and can't be explained separately. For example, when a Central American government announced a new federal budget that it said was going to both develop growth and reduce inflation, the numbers said that was a contradiction. You can't do both; you can do one or the other. You could only see that by dealing with both words and numbers.

I went on from there, in that book, to plow through the whole numbers thing as if everybody had a business plan event to worry about, and therefore a full complete formal plan to do. This was too much, in retrospect. You can track and manage most businesses with the core plan numbers in the sales forecast and the expense budget.

A business plan is like that, too. You can't describe a plan without both text and tables, both words and numbers. The single most important analysis in a business plan is a cash-flow plan, because cash is the most critical element in business. With the way the numbers work, however, you can't do a cash-flow plan without looking at the income statement and the balance sheet as well.

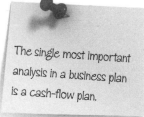

The single most important analysis in a business plan is a cash-flow plan.

You really can't do the income statement without looking at sales, cost of sales, personnel expenses, and other expenses, so you need those, too. And you'd have trouble doing a sales forecast without understanding your market, so a market analysis is recommended.

And then you have the break-even analysis as part of the initial assessment, and tables for business ratios, general assumptions, and other numbers. Step-by-step, the business plan becomes a collection of tables and charts around the text.

Although cash is critical, people think in terms of profits instead of cash. We all do. When you and your friends imagine a new business, you think of what it would cost to make the product, what you could sell it for, and what the profits per unit might be. We are trained to think of business as sales minus costs and expenses, which results in profits.

Unfortunately, we don't spend the profits in a business. We spend cash. Profitable companies go broke because they had all their money tied up in assets and couldn't pay their expenses. Working capital is critical to business health. Unfortunately, we don't see the cash implications as clearly as we should, which is one of the best reasons for proper business planning. We have to manage cash as well as profits.

Working capital is critical to business health.

This is all important, when you're doing the formal plan for outsiders. With the initial plan-as-you-go plan, some of it can wait until later.

We're going to address all of it in this book, by the way, but some of it waits for the business plan event, so you do it when you really need it, as your business and plan grow.

Separate Supporting Information from the Plan

One of the most important new ideas in the plan-as-you-go business plan is that the plan doesn't necessarily include the supporting information that everybody assumes is part of the traditional formal business plan. I mean the market analysis, industry analysis, company history, management team backgrounds, and other information you expect in a complete business plan.

Your plan is about what's going to happen, what you are going to do. It's about business strategy, specific milestones, dates, deadlines, and forecasts of sales and expenses and so forth.

So what about market analysis? Think about the business purpose. Do you need the market analysis to help determine your strategy? Then do it. Are you ready to go with that strategy regardless? Then don't sweat the market analysis.

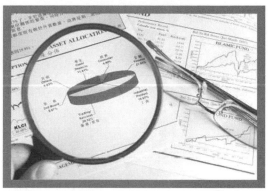

© Williv/iStock photo

Supporting information may or may not be included. You don't have to do a rigorous market analysis as part of your plan if you know exactly what you're offering and to whom.

This is ultimately your responsibility. You don't gather all the supporting information just because somebody said it is supposed to be there. You do it if you're going to actually use it to make decisions.

A Big Win

This is a big win for the plan-as-you-go business plan over the stan-dard traditional business plan. It helps preserve the idea of planning for the people who know what they're doing in the market, and who already know their industry, their customers, and their strategy and how and why it works, but don't plan because they think, wrongly, that doing a plan means proving something to somebody else. If you already know and you're satisfied with it, then skip the proof—but not the planning.

© Tina Spruce, Amanda Rohde/iStock photo

Inside Out from the Heart

You build a good plan like an artichoke, inside out *from the heart*. That doesn't mean you necessarily start with the heart and go in rapid succession—I am serious about starting *anywhere*—but it

MYTH BUSTER

THE PLAN IS WORTH THE DECISIONS IT CAUSES

A plan is worth the decisions it causes. If you already know your market, don't waste time or money doing market research.

Don't do it just because somebody said it was part of a business plan. But are you sure you know your market? Is it worth a fresh look? You decide.

The supporting information isn't part of your plan; it's just supporting information. Do you have to prove the concept? Will outsiders be reading your plan and evaluating it? Does the market research prove something that must be proven? Then include it.

Information in business is worth the decisions it causes. You measure this by taking a guess at what your bank balance would have been without the information and comparing it with what it is because you had the information. Subtract the balance with information from the balance without, and that's the value.

With the information:	$10,000
Without the information:	$8,000
Value of the information	**$2,000**

That's a hard equation to deal with sometimes, and of course it's based on hypothetical values, but it's still an important concept to understand. Your business plan shouldn't include anything your business won't use. Either it's going to use the market analysis or it needs to present it as proof of market for outsiders—or you just don't perform the analysis.

might. Maybe you did your sales forecast first, but eventually your plan will revolve around its heart.

Of course the heart is not necessarily a written document, not necessarily rehearsed, not necessarily recorded.

At this point, however, we have to address those of you who have a business plan event that you need to prepare for. You need a formal, complete plan for school, for an investor, for a bank, for a boss, as a consultant, or whatever. Then you might have to do the whole thing at once, and not enjoy the luxury of letting it grow organically. Don't worry, though: you can still benefit from the idea of the core and the blocks.

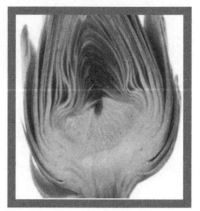

The artichoke analogy applies when you build the supporting parts of the plan—or blocks, if you want to call them that—around the heart. For example:

- A really cool way to make sure your planning is useful is to set up the review schedule now, in the beginning. Set up recurring meetings, for example, on the third Thursday of each month. Put these meetings on the calendar. Invite the team members. Surprise people; don't wait until the plan is done—set up the review schedule first.
- After you've figured out your market strategy, target market, focused offering, core competence, and so on, then you need to think through the logical tactics and specific activities to take that idea to market. What is the message? Where do you deliver it, to whom, through what medium? How much will that cost? You can do that with a strategy pyramid, or not; a milestones table is really practical.
- A lot of core benefits of planning link to the milestones table. Metrics, for example, are presumably built into that table. Tracking and accountability also relate to that table so it's a pretty important block.
- You really need to take your business strategy and work it into a concrete and specific sales forecast. Hard as forecasting might be, it's harder to run a business without it. And the

sales forecast is when you start tracking. Plan vs. actual numbers will help you adjust your plan, and from that improve your management.

- You need an expense budget. That's another piece you can track, so set up your goals and keep an eye on your progress. And while you're at it, include costs as well as expenses (see page 156) and you'll have a better hold on your business.

And with that, I want to pause. Take a breath. Notice that at this point you've got a strategy and three key metrics to track: milestones, sales, and spending. You're on your way. Your planning has started. You even have a review schedule.

All of these things are like the leaves of the artichoke. They surround the heart. They aren't the only things you can do, though; they are just suggestions. Here are some additional ideas:

- I like the SWOT analysis. It brings the teams together.
- Lots of people like to do the mission statement, or the mantra, or objectives. I like keys to success, too.
- You have to be sensitive to your business, and your business's needs. Maybe distribution channels are important, so you set some milestones. Maybe product design, prototyping, or packaging is important, so you set some milestones.
- The more you have a group involved, the more it helps to create a document on the computer. A set of bullet points, or maybe some prose, gets the ideas down so people can refer back to them.

And now another pause. Let's reflect on progress and process. A lot of this thinking things through, necessary for good business and good management, ends up in the milestones table.

- Is this plan going to be a document? I hope you see clearly now that it depends on needs. If you're going to show this document to somebody else, and you expect her to read it, then you might have to start writing things down and organizing things like outlines and structures. The milestones table won't explain itself.

- And even if it's just for your team members, although you will spend less time sweating the output details, you still probably want to record key points (Business Plan Pro software comes to mind, but it's not required) so people can refer to them.
- Form follows function. More on that later.

So this might be the evolution of a normal plan, for a normal company, startup or not. You do this plan not because somebody says you have to, but because you want to, because you're interested in creating a business or growing a business. You care about your business. You think about it a lot. Call it planning.

And then, in some cases, comes the business plan event. Or perhaps you're one of those who started this planning task with the full business plan event staring you in the face. No worry—in that case you add the dressing you need like the supporting information, detailed financial forecast, and descriptions of the management team, and you have the formal plan document.

Planning, Not Accounting

One of the most common errors in business planning is confusing planning with accounting.

They are two different dimensions. Accounting goes from today backward into time in ever-increasing detail. Planning, on the other hand, goes forward into the future in ever-increasing summary and aggregation.

One of the most common errors in business planning is confusing planning with accounting.

Understanding this difference helps you work with and understand the educated guessing you need to do to work projections—specifically, the sales forecast, expense forecast, and even-

MYTH BUSTER

BUSINESS PLANS ARE ALWAYS WRONG—BUT VITAL

It's a simple statement: all business plans are wrong, but nonetheless vital.

Paradoxical, perhaps, but still very true.

All business plans are wrong because we're human, we can't help it, we're predicting the future, and we're going to guess wrong.

But they are also vital to running a business because they help us track changes in assumptions and unexpected results in the context of the long-term goals of the company, long-term strategy, accountability, and, well, just about everything the plan-as-you-go business plan stands for.

tually the profit and loss, cash flow, and the rest of the financial forecast—into your business planning.

Accounting has to be correct to the last detail. You use it to pay taxes. Forecasts in a business plan aren't correct, by definition (see the Myth Buster above).

Different Dimensions

I like to use the 1994 movie *Stargate,* starring James Spader and Kurt Russell, to illustrate the difference between planning and accounting. In the movie, some fictitious freak of nature opens up a strange, luminous gate between two dimensions. On one side of it is the world as we know it. On the other side, is a strange, alien world like nothing we've ever seen. I like the idea because it reminds me of the differenct dimensions that are planning and accounting.

If that strikes you as theoretical or conceptual, perhaps even a bit impractical, think again. This is important. It can save you needless headache and stress. It will help keep you in the right dimension, understanding that the financial projections in your business plan are not meant to be built in excruciating detail.

A Simple Example

Take the balance sheet in Figure 2.3, a sample taken from Wikipedia. The so-called balance sheet is a standard financial report, listing

the assets and liabilities and capital of a business at the end of some specific day, month, year, or whatever. Assets are good—things you own, like cash and land, or money owed to you, like accounts receivable. Liabilities are debts, money you owe, which is why you see things that are "payable"—meaning you're going to have to pay

Sample Small Business Balance Sheet[9]			
Assets		**Liabilities and Owners' Equity**	
Cash	$ 16,600	Liabilities:	
Accounts Receivable	1,200	Notes Payable	$ 30,000	
Land	52,000	Accounts Payable	7,000	
Building	36,000	Total liabilities		$ 37,000
Tools and equipment	12,000	Owners' equity:	
		Capital Stock	$ 80,000	
		Retained Earnings	800	80,800
Total	$117,800	Total		$117,800

Figure 2.3 **Sample Balance Sheet**

them—as liabilities. Capital is what's left over. It's called a balance sheet because it's magic, the magic of double-entry bookkeeping: the assets are always exactly equal to the liabilities and the capital.

Is this an accounting report or a projection in a business plan? You can't tell. It looks exactly the same, either way. However, in truth, they are different dimensions.

Accounting Collects Records of Transactions

Accounting goes backward from today into the past in ever-increasing detail.

If it's accounting, then every number shown in a balance sheet is actually a summary report of a database full of transactions. The cash balance is like your checkbook balance; it's the result of adding up all the deposits and subtracting all the checks. What they call accounts receivable is the sum of all the amounts of money owed by all your different customers, a report of hundreds, maybe thousands, of different transactions. You make a sale, leave an invoice, wait to get paid, then finally get paid, record the transaction, debit cash and credit accounts receivable, and so on, through a collection of specific transactions. The $52,000 reported as land value might be what you paid for land, but it might be the resolution of dozens of land transactions, selling some, buying others, and that's the balance.

Accounting is a huge collection of summarized past transactions.

Liability balances, like assets, are built from the bottom up in accounting by keeping track of all the transactions and summarizing the end result. Notes payable might be dozens of small trade bills sitting on a spike somewhere, or a loan from the bank, in which case it's related to the starting loan amount less the total of all the principal payments.

I hope you get the idea: accounting is a huge collection of summarized past transactions. Focus on any number in an accounting statement and you should be able to zoom in on more detail, down to each individual transaction.

Planning Makes Reasonable Educated Guesses

Planning goes forward from today into the future in ever-increasing summary and aggregation.

Now consider, if you will, that same illustration as part of a business plan, making an estimated guess of what the balance will be two or three years from now. Don't even try, not for a second, to think that you're going to estimate cash by estimating the details of thousands of transactions and adding them up. You're not going to estimate assets by guessing what you're going to buy and when (not to mention depreciation, so pretend I didn't). You're not going to estimate debts by guessing when you will take out each loan, exactly what you will purchase, and when. That's impossible—and silly. You're going to find some way to guess your cash, your assets, and your liabilities based on larger educated guesses tied logically into the major flows, like sales.

We'll be working together later on how you can make reasonable estimates, but for the sake of illustration, I have some examples to explain the difference in dimensions:

Accounts receivable means money owed to you by customers.

- Accounts receivable means money owed to you by customers. You make the sale but you deliver an invoice and wait to get paid; that's the way it goes in business-to-business sales. So you need to guess how much money will be sitting there, at important points in the future, waiting to get paid. Every dollar in accounts receivable is a dollar less cash, because it was booked as sales but you don't have the money. You don't, however, try to guess all the specific sales transactions with all the specific customers and add them all up and figure out where the total will be two or three years from now. Instead, you guess what percent of sales involves invoices and waiting, and then you guess how many days on average you have to wait, and you can do some numbers tricks to make an educated guess.

■ You don't guess what you're going to owe by adding up all the imagined bills from some guessed-at future purchases. Instead, you estimate how much you're currently paying out in expenses as a percentage of sales and payroll or some other measure, then estimate about a month's worth of that as payables.

I'm not going to belabor the examples because I think that's already enough to make the point. You have to make some logical guesses.

Why Does This Matter?

Every so often I encounter somebody trying to manage the minute details of projected interest expense to allow for several different loans with differing rates and terms as part of a business plan. Or I find somebody trying to guess assets by guessing the detailed purchase dates and values. And then there are people trying to project future accounts receivable by customer, guessing each customer's future sales and payment patterns.

You can spend a lifetime calculating details and never get as close as you would with a good estimate.

The problem, of course, is that is really hard to do. You can spend a lifetime calculating details and never get as close as you would with a good estimate.

Compare the levels of certainty: Let's say interest is normally a percent or two of total expenses, and expenses are normally something like two-thirds of sales. If your sales estimate for future years is within 5 percent either way, you're doing way better than most. How wrong can you go with a simple estimated interest rate, and how much does that affect your projections? Aren't we talking about tiny percentages of expense, in a system that has to estimate other elements that have hundreds of times more uncertainty?

I consider this a problem of what I call levels of uncertainty, which is a matter of how correct you expect to be. For example, assume it's Spring of 2008. When your accounting report says your sales were $2,893,712.07 for 2007, and you put that number into your tax reports for 2007, you expect it to be absolutely correct. You have accounting software and professional accounting help, and you enter all the records, so you assume that the number is correct. That's presumably a very low level of uncertainty. Even a $10,000 difference between what you see on the accounting and what actually happened is very bad. On the other hand, when your 2008 business plan says you expect to sell $5 million for 2011, that's an educated guess with a relatively high level of uncertainty. While your accounting for past sales in a tax report is a disaster if it's off by even $10,000, your projected $5 million sales for three years from now has so much uncertainty to it that you're probably very pleased to end up within $500,000 of that 2008 planned number when you finally do get actual results for 2011.

Now take that same idea into more detail, using the example of specific interest expenses. Interest is deductible from income before you pay taxes, so if it's already 2008 then your accounting should be telling you down to the last penny what you paid in interest expense in 2007. Let's just take as an example that you paid $21,093.76 in interest for 2007. There is no margin for error. The interest expense for the whole year is the sum of all the separate interest payments paid for whatever different loans were involved. On the other hand, if it's 2008 now and you're estimating what your interest expenses will be in 2011, you can't possibly expect to be exactly right. And—most important—you should not try to calculate interest expenses in the future like you do for the past, by knowing all the loans you have and all the different interest rates and adding them all up. That kind of detail in projections just doesn't work. A simple estimate will do.

I suggest we think about this for just a second. Does it make sense that business planning is about projecting the future so exactly that using a simple average estimated interest rate applied to your projected liabilities isn't good enough? Do you really have time to be modeling the detailed impact of multiple hypothetical interest rates on multiple hypothetical loans as part of a projection that depends on an estimated sales forecast?

Planning is for making decisions, setting priorities, and management. Accounting is also for information and management, of course, but there are legal obligations related to taxes. Accounting must necessarily go very deep into detail. Planning requires a balance between detail and concept, because there are times when too much detail is not productive.

Good News: It Makes Things Easier

This is really good news for business planning. What it means is that you don't have to paint a picture of your financial future by detailing every brick in every building. You can do it with a broad brush. That doesn't make it less realistic; in fact, it will usually make it more realistic, at least that's what I've seen while working with thousands of people on thousands of business plans.

We're human. We work better at imagining the future in scale than at building it brick by brick in our minds.

A Final Word of Warning

Seeing the difference between planning and accounting is particularly hard for well-trained accountants to handle. They learned to build reports from the bottom up, from the detail, and it can drive them crazy when you make estimates using percentages and algebra and plain common sense for something they've learned to build up from painstaking detail.

More important than driving them crazy, unfortunately, is that sometimes this dimensional discomfort can make the accountants so unhappy that they'll say your estimates are wrong. In these cases, they are often misunderstanding what it means to be projecting the future in summary instead of counting the detail in the past. Forgive them—they mean well—but don't let them drive you crazy either. Stick to the planning.

It Has to Be Your Plan

"Please, can you recommend somebody to write my business plan for me? How much will it cost? How do I find somebody?"

"Where can I find (or buy) a business plan for a doggie day care? For a resort? For a website selling environmentally-sensitive goods?"

Forget it. You can't. It won't happen. Furthermore the whole idea of finding a ready-made business plan for your business is off-kilter. I think it's a new variation on the very bad idea of students buying term papers on the web instead of writing them themselves; and in this case, it's even worse, because it's not just a term paper that you should have done once.

It isn't something you just do and forget. It's your business plan. Your business is unique. Buying a business plan makes about as much sense as buying a medical checkup already done and on paper, instead of going to a doctor.

Your business is unique.

Many people confuse the idea of sample business plans with somehow getting a business plan that's already done. That doesn't work. Sample business plans can be useful in some cases because they can help you see what other people planned to do, in the best of cases in situations similar to yours. But their market is different from yours, their strategy is different, their resources are different, and their plan won't work for your business.

Businesses aren't built by recipes.

OK, there are some exceptions to these rules:

■ Sometimes a person with knowledge and experience in the right field can help you develop your business plan by asking

you the right questions and helping you think through your
ideas.

■ Sometimes when you need help creating a document from
your existing plan ideas, as long as the core content of the
document is yours, you can work collaboratively with somebody to actually craft the thoughts onto paper.

■ Most franchise businesses are formula businesses. The better
franchises do work like recipes. You follow the steps. In fact,
if it doesn't work like that, you aren't getting what you're
paying for as a franchisee.

More important, notice how the plan-as-you-go business plan
solves a lot of the stress related to finding a suitable existing business plan by focusing on doing only what you need, building it as
you go, and developing it as you need it, in pieces.

MYTH BUSTER

SAMPLE BUSINESS PLANS SUCK

The original title of this piece was "Business Plans Are Made, Not Found." It comes from
my childhood memories of the Wheaties ad campaign of the 1950s. The slogan was
"Champions Are Made, Not Found."

The same applies to business plans. You make one; you don't find one. You develop your own.

This idea comes up a lot these days because—I think—of sample business plans. The
spread of sample business plans is a real problem for the greater good of business planning. And unfortunately, I might be part of the problem. Gulp.

I started creating sample business plans at Palo Alto Software in 1987 with the first Business Plan Toolkit, which included the original versions of business plans for Acme Consulting and AMT, the computer reseller, which I had written for clients.

MYTH BUSTER

SAMPLE BUSINESS PLANS SUCK, CONTINUED

Digression: If you're curious, Google one or the other and see how widespread it is. By the way, there are a few sites that use one of these examples with permission (the SBA, for example, has permission to use AMT as a sample on its site), but there are a lot of people just copying one and calling it their own. Seems like there are hundreds of them out there. Only a very, very few have permission. Most are pirates. *End of digression.*

We came up with the idea of including sample plans with the business-planning product to help people understand what a business plan looks like, what it covers, and how it comes together. We included 10 real sample plans in late 1994 when we released Business Plan Pro. People liked the samples, so we included more. We polled the users and came up with 20 real plans from real businesses to include with our second version in February 1996, and 30 sample plans for the third version, in May 1998. People really liked sample plans as part of the product.

Then the idea spread. People started buying and selling sample plans. Our life as market leader became very complicated when a competitor bought 100-some sample plans from a book compilation and included them as Adobe PDF files with some business plan software. The company didn't tell its customers that the plans were just electronic documents, didn't work with their software, and most didn't even have financial information, but they did cause a stir in the market. We had to work like mad to get 250 real plans, all of which worked within Business Plan Pro and had financial data, to compete. We sponsored business plan competitions, and paid our customers, looking for real plans.

So the race was on. By this point we had our version 2002 (equivalent to fifth version) of Business Plan Pro out. People started selling sample plans on the web, most of them poorly disguised knockoffs of our sample plans exported from Business Plan Pro and massaged slightly. We've had several legal battles with people who used our work to compete against us. We're up to 500 sample business plans with Business Plan Pro now, and, frankly, I hate it.

MYTH BUSTER

SAMPLE BUSINESS PLANS SUCK, CONTINUED

Here's the problem: When it was two sample plans or even ten sample plans, people generally understood that the examples were supposed to give them an idea of what a plan is. Now with hundreds of sample plans available, some people naturally think their own business plan is supposed to be one of those 500.

As an author and professional business planner, I hate this idea. People are buying and selling finished business plans as if they were term papers (also a bad idea) for college students. The trend is really spreading, and it's a mistake. Not just wrong because of plagiarism, but wrong because it doesn't work and clouds business planning.

I get the question all the time: "Do you have a plan for X?"

This brings me back to the title of this sidebar. I want to tell everybody that finding a business plan you can use is a really, really bad idea. You make a plan; you don't find one. Obviously, every business is unique. Every business plan is unique. Even if you happened to find a plan for a business very much like yours, it would never have the same owners, the same management team, the same strategy, and probably not the same market or location either.

Sure, I recognize that a sample plan can help in several ways. You can find out how somebody else defined the units and prices in a business, what his expense projections were and for what categories, and how he described his market.

But I strongly recommend you start at zero and write your own plan. Refer to samples for some hard points, perhaps, but start with an empty plan. If you're using Business Plan Pro, the wizard takes you through the process step-by-step, and tells you what you need to include and why, so you just tell your own story and do your own numbers. If you start with somebody else's plan it's going to be very hard to distinguish your own ideas from hers. You're going to end up with a hodgepodge of rehash.

It's About Controlling Your Destiny

So it's not a hurdle. It's not a business plan document you have to finish before you do something else. It's an ongoing process, a regular management tool. You do it because you want to run your company well, move toward the future in an orderly fashion, dealing with change without always just reacting to change, sometimes proactively leading with change.

Business planning, particularly plan-as-you-go business planning, is the best way to control your own destiny. With a good planning process, you set your long-term goals and the steps to achieve them, then track progress carefully and watch changing assumptions and make corrections as needed

Don't Wait. Get Going.

© Habei Ren/iStock photo

IF YOU DREAD PLANNING YOUR STARTUP, DON'T START IT

Recently, I had one of those lightbulbs go off in my head. I'm referring to those times when you're reminded of something you already knew, but had forgotten. In my case, it was this: Planning your new business, the one you're thinking of starting, ought to be fun. Planning isn't about writing some ponderous homework assignment or dull business memo; it's

about envisioning that business that you want to create. It should be fascinating to you. What do people want, how are you going to get it to them, how are you different, and what do you do better than anybody else?

Honestly, isn't that related to the dreaming that makes some of us want to build our own businesses? It was for me, every time, including those ventures that made it and those that failed. Dreaming about the next thing I wanted to do was always part of it. Dreaming is related to looking forward, anticipating, and (in this case) business planning.

This idea came up one morning during my second day of video sessions for SBTV, which had been filming interviews with me on starting and managing a business and business planning. I was answering Beth Haselhorst's question, relating starting a business to getting out of the cubicle, when I realized that I was in danger of forgetting that business planning is part of the dreaming and part of the fun.

I think what's important is that none of us should be intimidated by business planning because of what I've called the not-so-big business plan, or the point I've made about starting anywhere you like. The business plan is a way to lay out your thoughts and think them through—it shouldn't be some dull, ponderous task you have to get through.

IF YOU DREAD PLANNING YOUR STARTUP, DON'T START IT, CONTINUED

If thinking through the core elements of your business, or for that matter the details of your business, isn't interesting, then get a clue. If you're not really looking forward to it, maybe you don't want to start the business after all.

If you dread the planning of your next vacation, stay home. If you dread the planning of your new startup, don't start it.

Adapted from an article originally published on the Up and Running Blog.

to move toward your long-term vision. You move as quickly as possible or as slowly as necessary.

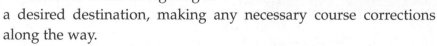

The opposite, not planning, leaves you and your business much more likely to become victims rather than drivers. You're much more likely to be reacting to the latest phone call, the latest problem, than managing a plan that makes you proactive.

Think of it like navigating to a desired destination, making any necessary course corrections along the way.

Do it for yourself, for your company, whether or not there is some business plan event that requires it. Do it because you care about your company and you want to make it better. Control your destiny.

TRUE STORY

MY WORST-EVER BUSINESS PLAN ENGAGEMENT

It's not for nothing that I always say a business plan has to be your plan and nobody else's. It can't be your consultant's plan. You must know it backward and forward and inside out, or it won't work.

I learned this the hard way, sitting in venture capital offices at 300 Sand Hill Drive, Menlo Park, California, the business plan consultant on the tail end of the new venture team. I had done the plan, built the financial model, written the text, shepherded the document through the painful coil binding and the whole thing, but I wasn't part of the team. I didn't want to be. I was still at grad school, getting my MBA, and my part of this venture was writing the plan, period. I needed the money to pay tuition.

In meeting after meeting, at key moments, the venture capitalists would ask critical questions and all heads would turn to me. I would answer. I knew the plan, backward, forward, and inside out, but I was the only one who did. It was my plan.

It was a good founders team. It included three Silicon Valley veterans—a marketing guy, a technical guy, and a deal-maker. They had about 40 years of computer company experience between them. They had a good idea and, much more important, a market window, differentiation, and the experience to make it happen.

© Duncan Walker/iStockphoto

The three of them never really got into the plan. It was a hurdle they paid me to jump for them. Every meeting generated new changes, so I would go back to the basement computer at the business school and rerun the financial model. The team of three didn't include a financial person to learn and manage the model, so it was always me doing the tweaking, which meant I was the only one who knew the plan. I'd rerun my financial model, edit the text, and publish a new version of the plan. They read paragraphs here and there, glanced at the numbers, but they stayed with the strategy and left the details to me.

TRUE STORY

MY WORST-EVER BUSINESS PLAN ENGAGEMENT, CONTINUED

Details that, in fact, they didn't look at. They trusted my faithful recording of their ideas and my financial modeling. They assumed, I guessed at the time, that these were functions that could always be delegated to somebody with special skills while they generated high-level strategy.

They did not get financed. I was disappointed. When you develop the plan and revise it dozens of times and support it and defend it through the long series of meetings with supposedly interested investors, you want it to take flight.

All these years later, memory of that disappointment is still fresh. I did learn my lesson, though, and I changed my strategy as a business plan consultant. From then on I made sure that any plan I worked on belonged—and I'm talking about intellectual ownership here, conceptual ownership—to the business owners, not the consultant.

If you have the luxury of a budget to pay an outside expert, consultant, or business plan writer, then maybe you should use one. This might be a good use of division of labor, and perhaps you can lever off somebody else's experience and expertise. However, that will not work for you unless you always remember that it has to be your plan, not the consultant's plan. Know everything in it, backward and forward, and inside out.

Adapted with permission from blog.timberry.com. All rights reserved.

Like Planning a Trip

Imagine that you're going to take the trip of a lifetime. You've got the time, you've got the money, and you're finally going to experience that dream trip.

Would you enjoy planning that trip? Would you browse the web with relish, looking at hotel reviews, airline guides, destination websites, and whatever else you could find? Would you browse the bookstore for guidebooks and maps? Imagine yourself sitting with your travel companion in your living room stashed with books and maps and telephone and computer, planning that trip. It's a good thought, right?

The heart of your plan is a combination of where you want to go, what you like to do, how, and with whom. The flesh and bones of your plan is a collection of concrete details: dates, flight numbers, hotel reservations, tour plans, and so on.

© Christine Balderas/iStockphoto

What would your travel plan look like? Where would you keep it? How would you share it?

You probably wouldn't write your trip itinerary out as a formal document with a prescribed outline, table of contents, and appendices. You probably would keep it where you could get to it quickly as needed, whether that was on your phone, on your laptop, or in a collection of papers in your carry-on bag.

And you probably would work with your plan as you took the trip. For example, as you travel, things happen. Flights get cancelled or delayed. You miss connections. The article in the in-flight magazine recommends a hotel or a restaurant you wouldn't have thought of otherwise. Hurricanes close airports. Hotels close for remodeling.

What do you do with your trip when things happen and circumstances change? You change your plan, you revise your schedule, you plan as you go. You sit somewhere with your travel companions and go back over guidebooks and schedules and possibilities, and you revise accordingly. You don't dump the core of your plan, but you might change the flesh-and-bones details.

You certainly wouldn't keep going as scheduled just because that original plan said so, right? You wouldn't try to fly into the hurricane or charter a plane to substitute for the one that was cancelled. You wouldn't sneak into the hotel that was closed for remodeling. You wouldn't ignore that great tip you got from the in-flight magazine.

Planning is part of the journey.

When assumptions change, you don't just run your head into a brick wall because that's what your plan said; you change your plan.

You enjoy the travel plan as you build it, and you revise and correct and improve the plan as you go. Take some guidebooks and maps and a laptop along, so you can change things later. Listen to people you meet who offer new ideas. Expect to revise your plan as things happen and assumptions change.

Planning is part of the journey. It makes it better.

You might call that plan-as-you-go traveling.

The Heart
of the Plan

The previous chapter suggests building a plan like an artichoke, with its heart in the center and the rest of the plan wrapping up and around it. It also suggests starting anywhere you like, which is a bit of a contradiction, or perhaps just another paradox. You can start anywhere you like, but build your plan around the heart, which implies that the heart comes first. And usually it does.

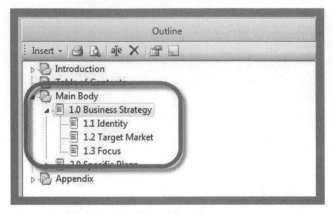

Figure 3.1 **The Heart of Your Plan**

The heart of the plan, which is also the heart of the business, is made up of a group of three core concepts that can't be separated: market, identity, and focus. Don't pull them apart. It's the interrelationship between them that drives your business. See Figure 3.1.

So let's look at what I call the heart of the plan-as-you-go business plan, the core strategy, which is this enmeshed combination of the business identity, the market element, and the strategic focus. I'm going to go through each of these in more detail in the rest of this section, but let's first establish that they are completely interrelated, and that you never separate any one of them from the other two.

Item	Description
Your Business Identity	This element is about you and your business, what I call your identity. How are you different from others? What are your strengths and weaknesses? What is your core competence? What are your goals?
Your Market	Telling the market story is about knowing and understanding your customers. Understand why they buy from you, what their wants and needs are, what business you are really in.
Strategic Focus	You can't do everything. In restaurants, you can't credibly offer great food at bargain prices with great atmosphere. If you say you do, nobody will believe you anyhow. So you have to focus. Make this focus intertwined and enmeshed with your choice of key target customer and your own business identity. All three concepts have to work together.

TIPS & TRAPS

BEFORE YOU
WRITE A BUSINESS PLAN

Validating the idea and understanding the business model are pretty important steps that should come before writing a business plan. That's hardly a novel idea.

Still, novel idea or not, successful entrepreneur Vivek Wadhwa spells out the early stages very well in a *BusinessWeek* special report published in early 2008, "Before You Write a Business Plan."

He starts with a short list for validating the idea:

1. Write down your thoughts on the product you want to build and the needs you want to solve. You'll be detailing your hypotheses.

2. Validate these hypotheses with as many potential customers as you can. Ask them if they will buy your product or service if you build it. Learn about what features they need and what they will pay for, ask them for more ideas, and be sure that there is a large enough market.

3. Build a prototype of your product or offer a test run of your service and again ask potential customers what they think about it. You'll find that customers usually provide much better input when they can actually try out a product.

Then Wadhwa also suggests a slightly longer list for developing the business model, by answering to a series of questions:

1. How are you going to find customers or have them find you? Are you going to advertise, cold-call, or rely on word of mouth?

2. How will you differentiate your product or service? There is always competition, so how are you going to set yourself apart?

3. What can you charge for your product or service that's profitable for you and provides value to the customer?

4. How are you going to persuade potential customers to buy from you? Even great products or services don't sell themselves; you have to develop a process for closing deals (*BusinessWeek*, 7/12/05).

**BEFORE YOU
WRITE A BUSINESS PLAN, CONTINUED**

5. How will you deliver your products or services to your customers? Are you going to have a direct sales force, sell through distributors, or sell over the internet? Can you do this cost-effectively?

6. How are you going to support your customers if your product breaks? Are you going to provide a telephone hotline, on-site support, or answer e-mails?

7. How are you going to ensure customer satisfaction and turn customers into loyal fans? Your success will ultimately depend on how happy your customers are.

These are good lists to go over as you consider your plan.

These three things are the heart of your business. Don't pull them apart. Don't take them one at a time. Don't ever stop thinking about them. Remember, in planning as well as in all of business, things change. Keep watching for changes in assumptions, in the environment, in your own team, or any changes that might affect your core or heart of the plan.

Your Business Identity

© Dean Turner/iStock photo

Although these three concepts are inseparable, we have to start somewhere, so let's look first at your business identity. This is what makes your business different from all others. What you want, what you do well, how you do things, what makes you unique.

What you want to do with your core strategy is establish that identity for yourself, your team, and out there in the market, for your customers.

Look at the Mirror

You have to understand what you do and who you are if you are going to be able to set your business apart from its competition. The exercise is something like looking at a mirror. Gather your team together, if you have a team ready, because this makes for a good discussion. Ask some of these questions:

- What do we like to do? How are we different? What is there about us that sets us apart? What excites us? What are we good at?
- What do we do that that other people (or companies) want to have done? What do we like to do that people want to pay for? What do we like to do that we do better or differently from others who do it?
- What value can we add? What's missing? How can we do something better than what's now available? What can we see about the future that others can't see?
- Where can we give value that isn't there right now?

Presumably, in whatever business you have or whatever business you're starting, you do something you want to do and believe in. Your team members have to want to do it and believe in it, too. That restaurant that is somebody's lifetime dream, or that skiing equipment shop, or that newsletter . . . success isn't based on the idea; it is based on how hard you've worked at creating your product or service, how much value you deliver.

In *The Art of the Start*, Guy Kawasaki offers a list of ways to generate new business ideas. If nothing else, read his first chapter. Kawasaki talks about getting going, about ideas being generated by impulses like "I want one" and "I can do this better" or "My employer wouldn't (or couldn't) do this." There too, it doesn't come out of the blue—it starts with you.

In *Growing a Business*, Paul Hawken shows how a business grows naturally out of the owners and founders doing something they want to do, filling a need they believe should be filled. I recommend reading that book also.

To be fair, there are exceptions. Franchise businesses, for example, when they work, follow a business formula that you pay for and implement, while being guided and taken by the hand every step of the way. Being a McDonald's franchisee means you're a millionaire; it doesn't mean you like eating or preparing what McDonald's restaurants serve. You buy a business to run. The franchisor tells you how to run it. If it isn't a set formula and if the franchisor doesn't give you all you need to know, then it's a bad deal.

Identify Your Core Competencies

To determine your core competencies, take another look at the mirror. Take a step away from the business, and get a new fresh look at it. What things do you do best? Let's consider a few companies most people know: We might reasonably think a core competency of Apple Computer is design, a core competency of Nordstrom is customer service, and a core competency of Volvo is vehicle safety. Figure 3.2 illustrates this idea: you have to recognize what you're good at. It can't be everything. You aren't credible if you try to do everything right.

You do have to understand your core competency as you develop your core strategy. Don't pretend you can be the best at service and have the lowest prices and the highest-quality

Figure 3.2 **Determine Your Core Competencies**

products; that isn't credible and it will just get in the way. Be honest with yourself or with your team.

Don't think that core competencies depend on the industry, or that they are the same for all players in any given industry. Look at the difference between economy cars, reliability cars, safety cars, and performance cars, for example. Or consider the different possibilities for a management consultant, whose core competencies might be any of these:

- Facilitation of discussions and brainstorming for the management team
- Cost cutting and firing
- Finding new growth opportunities in contiguous markets
- Finding people with money who can finance new ventures from the consultant's clients
- Developing documents that are easy to read and cover the bases well

And then consider the variations on food services and restaurants. To name just a few:

- Quick, fast, drive-through
- Excellent cuisine
- Ambience; good place for a date
- Sports bar
- Healthy fast foods

So this is not a difficult concept to understand. It usually leads to good discussion and a better sense of core strategy.

Mantra, Mission Statement, or Vision

People seem to like getting into the mission statement, but I'm not sure it's always such a good idea. There's also the possibility of doing your mantra instead, and people talk about a vision statement, and of course there are also business objectives.

TIPS & TRAPS

GUY KAWASAKI ON MISSION STATEMENTS
by Guy Kawasaki

The fundamental shortcoming of most mission statements is that everyone expects them to be highfalutin' and all-encompassing. The result is a long, boring, commonplace, and pointless joke.

In *The Mission Statement Book*, Jeffrey Abrams provides 301 examples of mission statements that demonstrate that companies are all writing the same mediocre stuff. To wit, this is a partial list of the frequency with which mission statements in Abrams's sample contained the same words:

- best—94
- communities—97
- customers—211
- excellence—77
- leader—106
- quality—169

Fortune (or *Forbes*, in my case) favors the bold, so I'll give you some advice that will make life easy for you: Postpone writing your mission statement. You can come up with it later when you're successful and have lots of time and money to waste. (If you're not successful, it won't matter that you didn't develop one.)

From: *The Art of the Start*

The underlying idea is sound: Let's think about who we are, what we want, what we want to do for customers, employees, and so forth. Let's use these words to define ourselves.

Before I go on, let's distinguish between these different items:

■ A mission statement should define what the business wants to do for at least three sets of people: customers, employees, and owners. It should not be just meaningless hype.

■ A mantra is a single phrase that defines a business. Kawasaki in *The Art of the Start*, recommends creating a mantra instead of a mission.

■ A vision statement projects forward into time three or five years and presents a picture, like a dream, of how things should be. Usually a vision statement works best as a story about the future, with your business as the key element in the story. Where it is, what it is doing, how big it is, what's special about it. This works for some businesses, but not all.

■ Business objectives should be hard-baked, concrete, specific, and above all, measurable. Objectives are like sales growth rates, employee head counts, customers in the database, percentages of gross margin or profitability, units sold, and so on.

Your mission statement is both opportunity and threat at the same time. It's an opportunity to define your business at the most basic level. It should tell your company story and ideals in less than 30 seconds: who your company is, what you do, what you stand for, and why you do it. It's a threat, however, because it can be a complete waste of time.

A mission statement is a complete waste of time when it's just meaningless phrases, hype that nobody can remember and wouldn't matter even if they could remember.

Most mission statements are essentially full of interchangeable, nice-sounding phrases like "excellence" and "leadership" that make all of them sound exactly the same. If you have a mission statement in your company, test it by asking yourself, honestly, whether your competitors could use exactly the same statement. Does it distinguish you from all other businesses? If you gave an employee or customer a blind screening test, asking him to read your mission

TIPS & TRAPS

MANTRAS VS. MISSIONS

We focus too much attention on mission statements. Too often they distract us from the real business of bearing down on why and how we're different, particularly when taken from the customers' point of view. The mission tends to be full of meaningless, fluffy words.

Here's a good test: Take your mission statement and ask yourself, honestly, if your competitiors' mission statements couldn't be exactly the same? Could one of your own team members guess which company was yours if he read your mission statement plus those of four competitors? Most companies' missions are full of promises about excellence and customer experience and leading-edge technology and such. They don't mean very much. Words like *excellence*, for example, mean nothing. Define *excellence*. Do you even know how?

Everybody writing a mission statement or even thinking about one ought to spend a few minutes online with the Dilbert Mission Statement Generator (at dilbert.com). Then read Guy Kawasaki's post "How to Change the World: Mantras Versus Missions" (at blog: guykawasaki.com). Pay special attention to how he suggests mantras might be more useful. This is from that post:

You should also create a mantra for your organization. A mantra is three or four words long. Tops. Its purpose is to help employees truly understand why the organization exists.

If I were the CEO of Wendy's, I would establish a corporate mantra of "healthy fast food." End of story. Here are more examples of corporate mantras to inspire you:

- Federal Express: "Peace of mind"
- Nike: "Authentic athletic performance"
- Target: "Democratize design"
- Mary Kay: "Enriching women's lives"

TIPS & TRAPS

MANTRAS VS. MISSIONS, CONTINUED

The ultimate test for a mantra (or mission statement) is if your telephone operators (Trixie and Biff) can tell you what it is. If they can, then you're onto something meaningful and memorable. If they can't, then, well, it sucks.

So why bother? Good question. Maybe the mantra is enough, as Kawasaki suggests. But some companies use their mission statements well; they do become part of the background of day-to-day work and long-term strategy development. For those cases, if you're really going to use a mission statement, then I say you should also remember three points a good mission statement should cover:

1. What are you doing for your customers?

2. What are you doing for your employees?

3. What does the company do for its owners?

If at this point you're still looking at developing a mission statement, then I recommend the basic guidelines beginning on the next page.

---

statement and four others without identifying which was which, would he be able to tell which mission statement was yours?

Consider the new trend, the idea of the mantra. Guy Kawasaki writes an eloquent argument for the mantra instead of the mission in his book *The Art of the Start* (see sidebar above). At the very least, think about it.

Before you do the mission statement, make sure you're going to use it. Will it actually set the underlying goals of the company? Will you refer to it as you develop and implement strategy? Will your team members know it, believe it, and use it in practice?

Then, start to ask yourself the most important questions. Do you want to make a profit, or is it enough to just make a living?

What markets are you serving, and what benefits do you offer them? Do you solve a problem for your customers? What kind of internal work environment do you want for your employees? All of these issues may be addressed in a mission statement.

Basic Guidelines in Writing a Mission Statement

Your mission statement is about you, your company, and your ideals. Read other companies' mission statements, but write a statement that is about you and not some other company. Make sure you actually believe in what you're writing; your customers and your employees will soon spot a lie. I suggest addressing three key components:

1. *What are you doing for your customers?* Let's hope this is something that sets you apart, that makes you different, and that your customers will recognize.
2. *What are you doing for your employees?* Fair compensation, good tools, professional development, encouragement, or whatever. If you're serious about it, put it in the mission statement. If it's in the mission statement, get serious about it.
3. *What does the company do for its owners?* Don't apologize for needing profits to stay in business, or for generating return on investment for those who invested. Say it as part of your mission statement.

A few more tips:

- *Don't "box" yourself in.* Your mission statement should be able to withstand the changes that come up over time in your product or service offerings or customer base. A cardboard box company isn't in the business of making cardboard boxes; it's in the business of providing protection for items that need to be stored or shipped. The broader understanding helps it see the big picture.

- *Keep it short.* The best mission statements tend to be three to four sentences long.
- *Ask for input.* Run your draft mission statement by your employees. Is it clear and easily understood, or does it sound like something from the Dilbert Mission Statement Generator (see dilbert.com)?
- *Aim for substance, not superlatives.* Avoid saying how great you are, what great quality and what great service you provide.

Keys to Success

Like the artist squinting to view the landscape better, or differently, as you build your sense of business identity, try to focus on keys to success. Keep it to just two or three key priorities that make the difference.

© Alex Bramwell/iStock photo

Some of these will depend on your industry, but there's a lot more to it than that. For food services, for example, you might think good food would be an obvious one, but what about a good location, easy drive-through, good parking, or even a proper match between price and reputation? Or marketing? Or the personality of the maitre d'?

In a retail business, for example, the classic joke is that the keys to success are location, location, and location. In truth, they might be, location, convenient parking, and low prices. It's different depending on your real identity, who you are as a business, and what your strategy is. A computer store's keys to success might be knowledgeable salespeople, major brands, and newspaper advertising.

This idea is related to core competence, but it isn't exactly the same thing. You hope you have core competencies that match your keys to success, but making that happen is a matter of working over time to build the business.

Use a SWOT Analysis

SWOT stands for strengths, weaknesses, opportunities, and threats. I particularly like the SWOT analysis because it's easy to understand and very quickly gets a team involved in strategic thinking.

In Figure 3.3, notice that there's a big difference between the first two and the last two components. Strengths and weaknesses are internal. They are part of your company identity. You can change them over time, but not easily; you have to work on it. Opportunities and threats are external. They are out there in the market, happening, whether you like it or not. You can't change them.

Especially when you're growing an existing business, you want the planning process to *pull your team together*, to develop commitment and accountability. Managers have to believe in a plan to implement it. They also have to believe that results will be tracked and that managers will be held accountable for disappointing results and will be given credit for positive results. Healthy planning process depends on everybody believing that results will make a difference. As an owner or operator of an existing business, recognize this team factor as a vital part of your planning process. Work on bringing the team into the planning at several levels.

Figure 3.3 **SWOT Analysis**

1. At least once a year, go through a strategy review process that begins with a SWOT meeting and SWOT review. Get your key people together and develop bullet points. Keep notes. Keep the discussion open.

2. Digest the results of the SWOT. Consider the responsibility that you have as owner or manager of a business, which involves some delicate balancing. On one hand, your plan should include your managers by reflecting their input. That's important for implementation. On the other, real business strategy can't be done by committee or popular vote. Sometimes a leader has to make hard and even unpopular decisions. So you should digest those SWOT results in a way that combines ownership responsibility with participation and teamwork. Optimize the SWOT. Sometimes that means that as you summarize the points made, you allow your summary to reflect and direct the discussion towards the strategy that you want to develop. This can be a difficult paradox to manage.

Keep in mind that strategy is focus.

3. Share the digested, optimized SWOT with your team of key managers. Develop the strategy. Keep in mind that strategy is focus, and remember the principles of long-term consistency, displacement, and priorities.

4. Give the team time to develop detailed strategy, tactics, and programs. You can use the strategy pyramid framework (see page 117), for example, to develop tactics to implement each of your strategy priorities and programs to implement those tactics. Keep everybody involved focused on strategic objectives.

5. Merge the team's contributions into a plan. Remember again that strategy isn't done by committee or popular vote. Somebody has to have the last word, and that somebody ought to the owner of the business.

6. Schedule regular implementation and plan review meetings—assign them dates and importance from the beginning—at the same time that you approve the plan. Make this schedule very specific, with real dates and times, so that every manager knows ahead of time; for example, meet on the third Thursday of every month. Review plan vs. actual results. Talk about why actual results are different from what was planned—and they always will be—and what should be done about it.

7. Make sure that those review meetings happen. They have to be important. If you're the owner, operator, or manager, make sure you attend and manage those meetings. If the review meetings fall apart, so will the plan.

During my 20-plus years as a business plan consultant and 10-plus more years running a company, I've seen many times how the SWOT can be an icebreaker. It invites people to contribute. It gets people thinking strategically, talking, sharing, and it turns a group of people into a team.

The SWOT also offers a good forum for opening up discussion. I've seen a SWOT discussion bring up problems that needed upper-management attention but might otherwise have remained hidden. Middle managers don't always like telling upper managers what's wrong. Even in a healthy company culture, that can be awkward. A SWOT analysis makes that easier.

For example, I once saw a 30-year-old software development manager suggest during a SWOT meeting that one company weakness was that the 50-year-old president kept messing with the software code instead of leaving it to the full-time pros. I attended another SWOT meeting in which several managers said ownership was unwilling to hold managers accountable for underperforming.

It's not magic. It's just an easy-to-understand framework that invites anybody who cares about a business to contribute.

Of course you have to manage a SWOT meeting well. Like any other meeting subject, SWOT can degenerate into useless discussion. A SWOT meeting should focus on the SWOT agenda and avoid unrelated side discussions. It should invite contributions without reprisals for negative comments. It's a variation on brainstorming, so contributions—as in suggested bullet points, suggested items on the list—are all positive as long as they are well-intentioned.

If you accept all comments, good and bad, you also get the benefit of bringing people into the discussion. Implementation is much more likely when managers contribute to the plan. They understand the background and they feel like the plan reflects their input. So use the SWOT both ways—use it to catalyze team commitment and to develop strategy.

SWOT Analysis is adapted from *Hurdle: The Book on Business Planning.*

Your Market Story

Telling your market story isn't about doing formal market research, or gathering the supporting information you'll need to include in a plan for investors, or professors, or in some cases for the bank, your boss, partners, or any other third-party plan judge or reader. No. This is about knowing your market for yourself, so that you understand the decisions you make, understand the strategy, understand the heart of your plan.

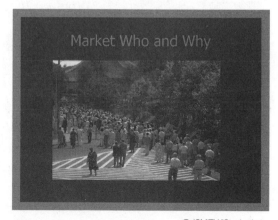

Market Who and Why

© ICMITU/iStock photo

You might get it from some kinds of market research, but in most cases we're talking about understanding the market. Understand what people want, or need, and why they buy from you. Understand what they think about when they think about your business.

For example, let's say you're in the restaurant business. Position yourself. Is your restaurant about fine food and fine dining? White tablecloths and wait people dressed up in black and white, a vase of flowers on each table? Or is it about driving through with half a kids soccer team in the van, getting a bunch of hamburgers and drinks and french fries fast?

What needs are you solving? Why do people buy from you?

Now imagine you're a business plan consultant. Can you do detailed market research for high-budget situations, like major companies looking for information about entering new markets? Or are you aiming at the people next door trying to start a business? Do you want buyers who expect to pay tens of thousands of dollars, and can you give them what they expect to get? Or are you aiming at those people who are borderline between having somebody do it and doing it themselves, who would pay $500 to get a plan done, but not $1,000? These are huge differences.

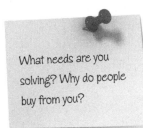

What needs are you solving? Why do people buy from you?

Now pretend you're running a blog. How and why will people find your blog, and what will make them return?

Imagine a conversation between your favorite customer and a friend or acquaintance, about your business. What do they say? "It's pricey, but the food is fabulous so it's worth it," or "It's a price performer. Not bad if you're in the neighborhood"?

One of the sadder elements of this exercise is the many businesses who don't really know how their market sees them. The bed-and-breakfast places who are getting customers because the hotels are full, whose customers wish the organizer woman would leave them alone. The bed-and-breakfast who is aiming for quaint and historic and full of character and is getting business because of location and low price. How sad when people change their formula without even realizing what, in their customers' minds, their formula was.

One of the best exercises is thinking through who isn't in your market. Who aren't you trying to reach? How does ruling that person out help you understand who you are looking for?

For example, Starbucks has to know that it isn't trying to get the drive-through customer in a hurry. The sushi restaurant has to know that a minivan carrying one parent and six 12-year-old kids in soccer uniforms isn't its market. The personal shopper has to know she isn't looking for cost-conscious bargain-basement buyers.

I Mean It Literally: Tell a Story about Your Target

I mean that you should tell a story, literally. Make the story about a single person, either a customer or consumer of your business or a decision-maker in a company that's part of the target market. Talk about who this person is. Give the customer a gender, an age, a family situation, and a problem to solve or a need or a want. Make it rich in detail. For example:

> *John Jones doesn't particularly care about clothes, but he knows he has to look good. He sees clients every day in the office, and he lives in a ritzy suburb, where he often sees clients by accident on weekends. But he hates to shop for clothes (The Trunk Club).*

> *Jane Smith wants to do her own business plan. She knows her business and what she wants to do but wants help organizing the plan and getting the right pieces together. The plan needs to look professional because she's promised to show it to her bank as part of the merchant account process. (Business Plan Pro)*

> *Paul and Milena live in a beautiful apartment in Manhattan, with their two kids. Paul has a great job in SoHo, Milena*

© James Steidl/iStock photo

works from home, and neither has time for food shopping. (Just Fresh)

Acme Consulting has five people managing three shared e-mail addresses: info@acme.com, sales@acme.com, and admin@acme.com. The five of them have trouble not stepping on each other. Sometimes a single e-mail gets answered three or four times, with different answers. Sometimes an e-mail goes unanswered for days, because everybody thinks somebody else has answered it. (EmailCenter Pro)

Notice that in each of these examples I could be much more general. The Trunk Club targets mainly men who don't like to shop but need to dress well and have enough money to pay for the service. Business Plan Pro is for the do-it-yourselfer who wants good business planning. EmailCenter Pro is for companies managing shared e-mail addresses like sales@ or info@. But instead of generally describing a market, I've made it personal.

Sometimes you can get away with generalizing. "Farmers in the Willamette Valley," for example, or "parents of gifted children." It's an easy way to slide into describing a market. However, I suspect that you're almost always better off starting with a more readily imaginable single person and letting that person stand for your target market.

Profile Your Ideal Customer

John Jantsch, in *Duct Tape Marketing*, recommends that you start by profiling your ideal customer. Focus for a while on one person, whether he or she is your customer directly or the decision-maker for a business customer. Give that person age, gender, income level, likes, dislikes, favorite movies, songs, magazines, restaurants. Know that person.

If you've been in business, you can think of that customer fairly easily. Maybe it's a composite of several real customers. What you want at this point is to be able to tell a story about this customer and his or her needs and wants and how your business addresses them.

Understand Needs and Wants

Clean your mind for a few minutes. Forget how great what you're selling is. Forget the features you've focused on and your marketing literature. Think about what your customer wants. Why does he buy from you?

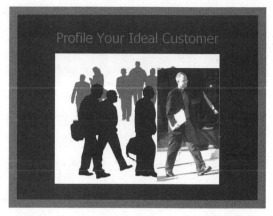

© A-digit/iStock photo

Think about Starbucks for a minute, a brand most people know. Starbucks doesn't think it's selling coffee drinks. Starbucks sells affordable luxury. Starbucks sells atmosphere, a place to meet.

Then consider two different options for selling food. One of them is selling convenience, reliability, consistency; it's a great solution for a parent driving a van full of kids in soccer uniforms, kids that the parent needs to feed between games.

© Amanda Penton/iStock photo

The other is selling luxury, atmosphere, fine food and peace and quiet, a fancy meal for a date—in short, something completely different from the first "product."

Now go back to your target customer, and think about that story. Who is this, what situation is she in, why

© Lisa F. Young, Allan Johnson/iStock photo

does she pay you money? What are you really selling? What business are you really in?

The Fresh Look

Back in the 1970s when I was a foreign correspondent living in Mexico City, I dealt frequently with an American diplomat who provided information about Mexico's increasing oil exports, which were a big story back then. We had lunch about once a month. He became a friend.

Then one day he told me he was being transferred to another post because he had been in Mexico too long. "What? but you've only been here for three years," I said. I was disappointed for two reasons—losing a friend and losing a source of information. "You've barely learned the good restaurants!"

Take a "fresh look" at the market at least once a year.

He explained to me that the U.S. Foreign Service moved people about every three years on purpose. "Otherwise we think we know everything and we stop questioning assumptions," he said. "That's dangerous."

I remember that day still because I've seen the same phenomenon so many times in the years since, in business. Business owners and operators are so obviously likely to fall into the same trap. Our business landscape is constantly changing, no matter what business we're in, but we keep forgetting to take a fresh look. "We tried that and it didn't work" is a terrible answer to a suggestion when a few years have gone by since it was first mentioned. What didn't work in 2000 might be just what your business needs right now. But you think you don't have to try again what didn't work a few years ago.

This is why I advocate taking a "fresh look" at the market at least once a year. Existing businesses that want to grow too often skip the part of business planning that requires looking closely at their market, why people buy, who competes against them, what else they might do, what their customers think about them. Think of the artist squinting to get a better view of the landscape. Step back from the business and take a new look. Use standard market research techniques and content just apply it to your business, not a new opportunity.

Talking to customers—well, listening to customers, actually— is particularly important. Don't ever assume you know what your customers think about your company. Things change. If you don't poll your customers regularly, do it at least once a year as part of the fresh look. As an owner, you should listen to at least a few of your customers at least once a year. It's a good exercise.

For creativity's sake, think about revising your market segmentation and creating a new segmentation. If, for example, you've divided by size of business, divide by region or type of business or type of decision process. If you've always used demographics, use psychographics.

Remember to stress benefits. Review what benefits your customers receive when they buy with you, and follow those benefits into a new view of your market.

Question all your assumptions. What has always been true may not be true anymore. That's what I call the fresh look.

The artist takes a fresh look at the scene every time he paints it. How many times has this man seen the banks of the Seine? It doesn't matter, because he sees it differently each time. You need to take a fresh look at your market and your strategic situation at least once a year.

© Gaffera/iStock photo

Who Isn't Your Customer?

Consider the Trunk Club, Joanna Van Vleck's interesting startup, described in "Startup Success Story: The Trunk Club" in Up and

Running at upandrunning.entrepreneur.com. How important is it that she understands who isn't her customer? She told me the following points herself:

- I realized that although I thought my target was women, women are normally closer to style. In general. So they aren't as likely to pay money for style consulting.
- Men have less ego invested. Some, in fact, pride themselves on not knowing style. In general.
- The metrosexual man is not my customer. He loves his own style and spends his own time and effort finding it.
- The man whose partner in a relationship likes to shop for his clothes is not my customer. She wants to do it. She doesn't want me to.
- The younger men on a budget aren't my customers. They can't afford me.

TIPS & TRAPS

JUMP TO THE FUTURE AND ASK THIS QUESTION

You fall in love with your plan, and love is blind. You don't see the fatal flaw.

I know a man who jumped headfirst into a new venture based on building a chain of used CD stores. The punch line? It was 2000. Napster was already there. Do you see the fatal flaw? He didn't. And this was a man who'd had a string of successes.

Love is blind.

So here's a trick that might, sometimes, if you're lucky, help you see the fatal flaw.

1. It takes imagination. So close your eyes, relax your shoulders, and take a deep breath and let it out slowly.

2. Jump in your imagination to the future. Go to three years from now.

TIPS & TRAPS

JUMP TO THE FUTURE AND ASK THIS QUESTION, CONTINUED

3. Now pretend that, there in the future, you know that the business you are starting now, your baby, your dream, is over. It failed. I know, that's hard, but it's a game; it's only in your imagination, so make that leap.

4. You're sitting at a table, maybe in a coffee shop, maybe at lunch, and somebody asks you: "What happened? Why did it fail?"

5. Now, using your imagination, your intelligence, and what you know about your business, answer that question. This is fiction now, so you have to tell a story. Make it believable. What happened?

© NielsLaan/iStock photo

This activity will help you think about flaws. Was it competition? Did the management lose interest? Was there not enough money? Did some new technology come along?

I don't know for sure, but I believe that if my friend with the used CD stores had done this exercise, he would have come up with the possibility of a change in the way we deal with music, meaning Napster, downloading, iTunes, and so on.

And, for the record, I haven't done the research, either, but what do you think? Would you like to own a used CD store? What do you think has happened to the sale of used CDs?

Adapted from Up and Running blog.

Notice how the "isn't my customer" routine helps define and position your marketing better.

A fast-food restaurant knows that the relatively well-to-do baby boomer empty nesters aren't its customers. On average. The sushi restaurant knows that the construction worker driving a pickup truck who eats at the Texas barbecue drive-through isn't its customer.

Consider Jolt cola. Twice the sugar and twice the caffeine. How important is understanding who isn't the customer.

Your blog, if you're running a blog as a business, needs a focus. People don't care about your inner angst, but there are specialty niche areas all over the place. Old Volkswagen maintenance. Arranging dry flowers. The narrower you cut it, the better. Sure there are some general blogs that work, but they started years before you did. Nowadays you need to focus.

Strategic Focus

Strategy is Focus

© Kiss Botund/iStock photo

Some people make a big deal about business strategy. The Amazon.com search for books about business strategy is daunting. People do doctoral theses on it and then they charge huge fees to help huge companies figure out strategy.

But this is the real world. Your business. And when you pull it back down out of the ivory tower, the good strategies are usually pretty obvious. Some would say boring.

Your strategy pulls in both identity and market.

- On the identity side of things, you want to focus on strengths and away from weaknesses. You want to take advantage of your core competencies.
- On the market side of things, you want to focus on a well-defined target market so you can tailor your message and your business offering. You don't want to be just a restaurant; you want to be a restaurant with a focus that fits a target market, with price, food, and ambience to match. You don't want to be just a market research and planning consultant; you want to be a market research and planning

consultant with a focus on personal computer markets in Latin America.

As I've said elsewhere, your focus is intimately related to your identity and your market. You cannot pull these enmeshed concepts apart.

> "I don't know the secret to success. But I do know that the secret to failure is trying to please everyone."
>
> —BILL COSBY

Growth vs. Focus

It is paradoxical. If you stay focused on the key elements of your business, you aren't looking at new opportunities. That's one of the reasons that strategy is done by humans, not by recipes or algorithms. It takes a human to deal with the paradox and complexity.

Business strategy often involves tough decisions. Do you focus on what you know well, and consolidate, build on your core competencies? What if the market changes or technology changes and leaves you behind? But if you constantly move into new areas, constantly pursue new opportunities, you run into the problems of displacement and long-term inconsistency.

Deal with it. That's why you are in charge. You make the tough decisions.

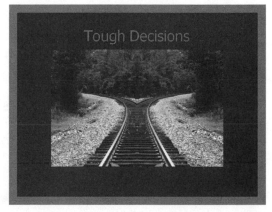

© Kelly Talele/iStock photo

Understand Displacement

Displacement: In the real world of small business, everything you do is something else you can't do.

Understanding displacement is vital for business planning, vital for growing a business, vital for small- and medium-businesses in particular. Consider Figure 3.4, showing marbles dropping into a full glass of water. The water comes splashing out of the glass and

GENERAL PRINCIPLES OF REAL-WORLD STRATEGY

In 30 years of working with businesses of all sizes, I've come across several of what I would call general principles of strategy. These don't necessarily apply in the academic world, or for larger corporate enterprises, but they do apply to small and medium businesses everywhere.

- *Strategy is focus.* The more priorities in a plan, the less chance of successful implementation.

- *Strategy needs to be consistently applied over a long term to work.* Better to have a mediocre long-term strategy consistently applied for years than a series of brilliant but contradictory strategies that never last long enough to matter.

- *Strategy needs to be tailored.* There are no standard strategies. Every company is different. A given strategy must always be tailored for a specific company.

- *Strategy needs to be realistic.* You have to deal with your company as it is at this point in time, understanding what choices you really have, what knobs you can actually turn.

- *The best strategies are market driven.* When possible, it's not "how to sell what we have," but rather, "how to make what people want or need what we offer."

- *Good strategies understand displacement.* Displacement in business refers to the undeniable fact that everything you try to do rules out many other things that you therefore can't do. You have to choose carefully, because one project displaces many others.

From *Hurdle: The Book on Business Planning.*

onto the table. That's a good illustration of displacement and how it works in business.

I've seen it so many times: trying to plan their business, people start making lists of things that ought to be done and end up with huge, unrealistic and impossible business plans because they haven't come to terms with displacement.

Learn to live with the reality of displacement and you'll do better planning your business and, particularly, growing your business.

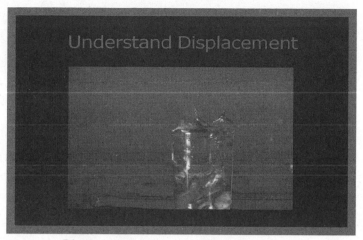

Figure 3.4 **Displacement**

What Knobs Can You Turn?

A good way to keep your planning realistic is to know what knobs you have to turn.

For example, say you're working a tractor, trying to dig out a boulder in the middle of your yard or field. What knobs (for controls) do you have to turn?

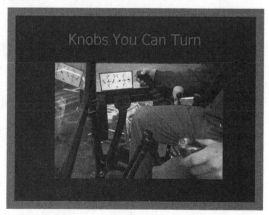

- You have controls to move the tractor forward, move it backward, and turn it.
- You have controls to go faster or slower.
- You have controls to deal with the tractor equipment, like the blade and the digger.

© Andy Hill/iStock photo

And those knobs are your universe of solutions. So you deal with your problem given the controls you have. It doesn't do you any good to think about what you'd like to do if you don't have a control that can do that.

This is an important concept to keep in mind in business. You might want a lot of things for your business, but if you don't have the resources to get there, if you don't have the right people, or the know-how, or the working capital, then you have to plan on getting the resources first.

Strategy has to be realistic. Know what knobs you have to turn. Keep it real.

Strategy Is Tailored to Your Size

© Jorge Oliveira/iStock photo

Forget finding a strategy for a certain type of business or following somebody else's strategy. It won't work. Strategy has to be unique, tailored to your business. You have your own identity, including strengths, weaknesses, goals, core competencies. You have to develop your strategy, for your company.

This should be obvious, but some people still try to find *the* strategy for a restaurant, or a management consultant, or whatever.

Remember: Your Plan Is Not Necessarily a Written Document

I want you to use words and numbers written down somewhere to keep track of your plan, but that doesn't mean it isn't there unless you have it written into a text. It is there if you know it and if your team knows it.

Don't get freaked out by the text or the writing. It's just for you, and probably your team members, to track your progress. Just type snippets. Stream of consciousness is fine. Pictures, photos, or charts are fine, too. Some of my favorite plans use illustrations or pictures to represent the key concepts for the heart of the plan; they can be as simple as a single slide.

TIPS & TRAPS

THE BUSINESS MODEL

Nobody talked much about business models until suddenly a lot of businesses, valued for a lot of money, didn't have them.

For almost any traditional business, the business model is so obvious that you don't have to talk about it. Stores sell goods. Restaurants sell meals. Hotels sell lodging. Airlines and taxis sell transportation.

Think of the business model as how you make money—how you get money out of your customer's pocket and into your bank account.

The new businesses, mainly web businesses, need to explain how they make money. Some of the most highly valued businesses in the world—Facebook, for example—don't have an obvious way to make money.

Some businesses still get away with generating traffic, so-called eyeballs, but not money. The underlying assumption in these cases is that the traffic means a likelihood of being able to generate money somehow, someday.

And if you want to be really trendy, use the phrase *business model* to mean type of business. This can get really interesting. Take a look at Alexander Osterwald's Business Model Design and Innovation, for example, a blog focusing on new ways to do business. Here's how he defines the business model:

TIPS & TRAPS

THE BUSINESS MODEL, CONTINUED

A business model is a conceptual tool that contains a set of elements and their relationships and allows expressing the business logic of a specific firm. It is a description of the value a company offers to one or several segments of customers and of the architecture of the firm and its network of partners for creating, marketing, and delivering this value and relationship capital, to generate profitable and sustainable revenue streams.

Along with that he adds nine points:

1. The *value proposition* of what is offered to the market;

2. The *target customer segments* addressed by the value proposition;

3. The communication and *distribution channels* to reach customers and offer the value proposition;

4. The *relationships* established with customers;

5. The *core capabilities* needed to make the business model possible;

6. The *configuration of activities* to implement the business model;

7. The *partners* and their motivations of coming together to make a business model happen;

8. The *revenue streams* generated by the business model constituting the revenue model;

9. The *cost structure* resulting of the business model.

This is perhaps a bit thick in language, but still, a nice summary of a business. You could use this as the heart of a plan too, no? His value proposition is our business offering, his target customer segment is obvious, but our strategy adds more attention to your business identity and your narrowed strategic focus. This is descriptive. Regardless, it's a good list.

Sometimes it's as simple as a mantra: Fine dining in Eugene, Oregon. Fresh organic Korean food in lower Manhattan. Your weekend cottage in Cape Cod. Healthy fast foods.

You might be writing bullet points. Whether short text or picture or completely written out discussions, you want to keep track of your plan so you can review and revise it and, of course, communicate between different people. But until you need to present it as a document to be read by others, don't make extra work. Keep it simple.

I do recommend keeping it on a computer, making it accessible to the few key team members who must be able to refer to it, but do only what you need.

Flesh and Bones

I like to think of defining flesh and bones as setting the steps. You have a strategy, you've got the heart of your business settled, but you want to set it down into concrete steps you can follow and track. To follow up on a plan and turn it into effective management, you have to have specifics that you can track and manage. This turns a plan into a planning process, and it makes for management. This chapter deals with the

© Malcolm Romain/iStock photo

specific steps you can take to make things happen. Remember: Good business planning is nine parts implementation for every one part strategy.

So here's what's in this chapter.

Item	Description
Action Plan: What's Going to Happen? When?	It centers on the milestones table, a simple, specific plan for what's supposed to happen, with start dates and end dates and responsibility assignments.
	It also includes the following tasks:
	• scheduling regular reviews of the plan
	• identifying assumptions
	• developing metrics: leaving tracks
	• planning the business activities: what to do when
Basic Business Numbers	Don't miss the opportunity to manage your business by running plan vs. actual analysis on some key numbers. It's not necessarily the whole big (scary to some) financial forecast, but
	• you should have a sales forecast—that's really central to tracking progress;
	• you should also manage an expense budget—it's something else you can track to improve management;
	• if and only if you're starting a business, then you want to have your startup costs figured out; and
	• whatever else you're doing, you should be aware of the cash traps.

Action Plan: What's Going to Happen? When?

I call it an action plan, but in some ways that's just another buzz-word. The real flesh and bones of your plan is what's going to happen, when, who's going to do it, how much it is going to cost, and how many sales it will generate (see Figure 4.1). Strategy is nice, but the real plan-as-you-go business plan is about specifics that you can track and manage. And that's the flesh and bones of the plan.

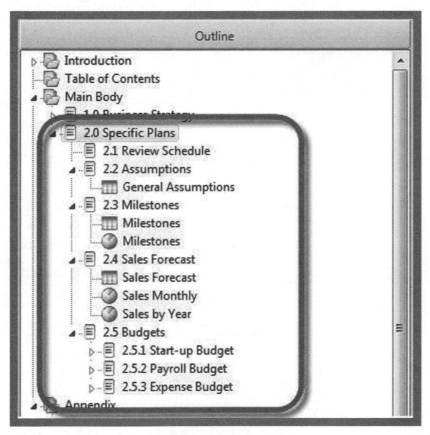

Figure 4.1 **The Flesh and Bones of Your Plan**

The Plan Review Schedule

Here's one element of the plan-as-you-go business plan that you won't see automatically on most other business plan outlines or formats: the review schedule.

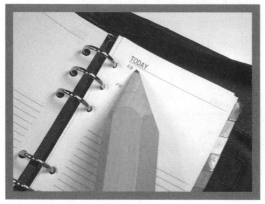

© Tom McNemar/iStock photo

One of the lesser known, but more important, facts about planning is that every business plan needs a review schedule. People have to know when the plan will be reviewed, and by whom.

For example, in Palo Alto Software we established the third Thursday of every month as the plan review meeting day. In the old days we brought in lunch and took over the conference room. It wasn't a big deal. We were done in 90 minutes. But we scheduled all the meetings as part of the next year's plan, and key team members knew they should be there and wanted to be there. Absences happened, but only when they were unavoidable.

I speak in the past tense only because after our United Kingdom subsidiary's managing director was added to the group, those lunch meetings became morning meetings. Our nine in the morning is London's five in the afternoon. Then in 2007 when the new management team took over, the review meetings moved to Wednesdays. But we still have them.

Remember, there's no reason to plan without plan review. I hope I've made that clear throughout this book. A few more tips:

- *Try to always start your review meetings with an initial discussion of key assumptions.* This is why I say elsewhere that it's so important to list those assumptions where they stay on top of mind.
- *Mind the discipline of keeping changes in strategy and changes in assumptions related to each other.*

- *Keep review meetings as short as possible*. One of the biggest threats to an efficient, effective planning process is spending too much time in meetings discussing the same things.
- *Emphasize metrics*. Focus on concrete, specific details. Metrics are most important. How do actual metrics compare to plan metrics. Variances, meaning the differences between plan and actual, should be discussed. The obvious metrics are the financial results, but don't let those be the only metrics (page 107).
- *Be keenly aware of the "crystal ball and chain" phenomenon*. The risk is that planning becomes a no-win game in which people commit to future metrics that come back to bite them. It's as if it were a management trick to hold over people's heads. Don't let that happen. Make sure planning is collaborative, so that it is always understood that change can happen and when it's managed, is good. Planning helps us manage change; it isnt really just to keep track of how bad we are at predicting the future. Remember, your business plan is always wrong.

Identify Important Assumptions

Identifying assumptions is extremely important for the planning process and the plan-as-you-go business plan. Planning is about managing change, and in today's world, change happens very fast. Assumptions solve the paradox between managing consistency over time and not banging your head against a brick wall.

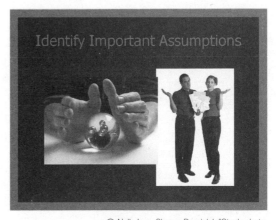

© Neils Lan, Sharon Dominick/iStock photo

Assumptions might be different for each company. There is no set list. What's best is to think about those assumptions as you build your metrics, including sales forecasts and expense budgets, and write them out as much as possible.

The key here is to be able to identity and distinguish between changed assumptions and the difference between planned and actual performance. You don't truly build accountability into a planning process until you have a good list of assumptions that might change.

Some of these assumptions go into a table, with numbers, if you want. For example, you might have a table with interest rates if you're paying off debt, or tax rates, and so on.

Many assumptions deserve special attention. Maybe in bullet points. Maybe in slides. Maybe just in a simple list. Keep them on top of your mind, somewhere where they'll come up quickly at review meetings.

Think about event assumptions. Or date assumptions.

■ Maybe you're assuming starting dates of one project or another, and these affect other projects. Contingencies pile up.

■ Maybe you're assuming product release, or liquor license, or finding a location, or winning the dealership, or choosing the partner, or finding the missing link on the team.

■ Maybe you're assuming some technology coming on line at a certain time.

■ You're probably assuming some factors in your sales forecast or your expense budget; if they change, note it, and deal with them as changed assumptions.

■ You may be assuming something about competition. How long do you have before the competition does something unexpected? Do you have that on your assumptions list?

For more examples, see Figure 4.2.

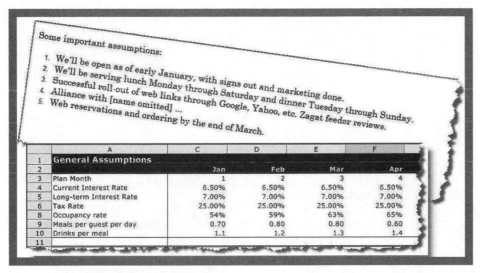

Some important assumptions:

1. We'll be open as of early January, with signs out and marketing done.
2. We'll be serving lunch Monday through Saturday and dinner Tuesday through Sunday.
3. Successful roll-out of web links through Google, Yahoo, etc. Zagat feeder reviews.
4. Alliance with [name omitted] ...
5. Web reservations and ordering by the end of March.

	A	C	D	E	F
1	**General Assumptions**				
2		Jan	Feb	Mar	Apr
3	Plan Month	1	2	3	4
4	Current Interest Rate	6.50%	6.50%	6.50%	6.50%
5	Long-term Interest Rate	7.00%	7.00%	7.00%	7.00%
6	Tax Rate	25.00%	25.00%	25.00%	25.00%
8	Occupancy rate	54%	59%	63%	65%
9	Meals per guest per day	0.70	0.80	0.80	0.60
10	Drinks per meal	1.1	1.2	1.3	1.4
11					

Figure 4.2 **Sample Assumption Lists**

Develop Metrics

Metrics are a critical element of the plan-as-you-go business plan. The planning process requires pulling people into the regular review schedule and helping them care about performance and results. For that, you need to develop metrics.

Recently I listened to an HBR Ideacast interview with Patrick Lencioni, author of *The Three Signs of a Miserable Job.* Here's a quote from the podcast:

> *All human beings in any kind of a job need some way to assess their own performance that's objective. It might not be numerical or easily quantitative, but it's somewhat objective and observable by them, because then they are not left to depend upon the opinion or the whim of a manager once a year during a performance appraisal. People need to be able to go home from work every night, or every week, or every month, and know where they stand, and know what*

THE MAGIC OF METRICS

I love metrics. Metrics in business means some specific set of numbers you measure and get measured by, ideally numbers that anybody can understand. You know you have metrics when you find yourself checking the numbers every morning, every day, or every hour.

© Juergen Sack/iStock photo

I think that's a good thing. It makes a game of it. You get a score. I'm a person who times myself when I run, and I run very slowly, but I still note whether it takes me more or less time on the days I do it. I like scores. I like to compete. I usually compete against myself and my past, but still, I like to compete.

When I was with United Press International in Mexico City, many years ago, every day when we came into the office we had "the logs" as a metric. The logs were a scoring of how many newspapers used our story and how many used the competition's (Associated Press) story. The logs were like a football score. If more newspapers used my story than the AP story, I'd won. Scores were like 12–7, 4–3, 20–1 . . .you get the idea. I still remember the one I won 23–1, a story about a mudslide. My lead was about people "buried in a tomb of mud," and the newspapers liked it.

Fast-forward to business today. Ideally, every person in the company has his own metric to watch. The CEO watches a bunch of them, of course, but the bunch is composed of lots of separate metrics. The customer service rep counts calls taken, or orders. The tech support rep counts issues resolved every day. The product development people watch returns, tech support issues per capita, and issue flow. The finance people watch balances, interest income, and margins. The online webmaster watches visits, pages, pay-per-click yield, orders, sales volume, and search placements.

My vision of a company working well is people checking and sharing their metrics. They are accountable for metrics and proud when they do well. The goals are built into the plan, and the

THE MAGIC OF METRICS, CONTINUED

actual results are compared against the plan regularly. The plan is reviewed and revised and the course is corrected based on, among other things, the metrics.

Of course the metrics have to be the right metrics. Don't track somebody on things he can't control, and don't accidentally use metrics to push the wrong buttons. For example, years ago I had a sales manager who was tracked on sales dollars alone, who also controlled expenses and pricing. Sales went up but margins went way down. That was predictable. Track a customer service agent on call volume alone, or a tech support rep on a number of issues handled, and customer satisfaction will suffer.

© Lisa Kyle Young/iStock photo

The metrics should also be built around a reasonable plan. They need to be aligned with the plan, so they tie directly into strategy.

And metrics have to be tracked. They are part of a larger planning process in which plans are kept alive and reviewed and courses are corrected as assumptions change.

These days I am particularly happy with the flow of the metrics in my job. Until recently I was responsible for the entire company, the CEO. My metrics were all over the map. Sales, profits, cash flow, unit sales, payroll, health, wealth, and the pursuit of happiness, all of which was pretty vague and hard to track. Today I'm still president, but my job is about teaching, writing, speaking, and blogging. And blogging gives me a single set of metrics (traffic, page views, subscribers, etc.) I can watch and enjoy, or suffer, every day. Like back in the old days, at UPI. That's cool.

Adapted from blog.timberry.com.

they can do to influence how they're working. This is why salespeople are generally very satisfied in their job, because they have very clear evidence of their performance. Most people think they are coin-operated, but in fact a quota is a wonderful scoreboard for them evaluating themselves, and all people need that.

Sometimes it requires a manager to be very creative in how they come up with that. In my book this one guy works at the drive-through window in a fast-food restaurant and the manager helps him realize that the best way he can measure the impact of his success is to find how many times he can make somebody smile or laugh that comes through his line. So he writes down or records for himself how often he can do that.

We have to give people that sense that they have some measure of control.

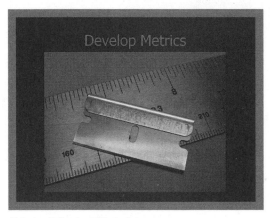

© Andrew F. Kazmierski/iStock photo

This is about metrics. Find ways to help people track progress toward goals. Build numbers into your plan so people can see their own progress, and peers can see each other's progress.

The most obvious metrics are in the financial reports: sales, cost of sales, expenses, and so on.

As you build your planning process, look for metrics throughout the business, aside from what shows up in the financial reports. It's different for every business and for every function in the business. For example:

- What about measuring sales beyond the sales numbers? How about what leads to sales, such as leads, presentations, or proposals?
- You can measure calls taken and minutes per call.

**TIPS &
TRAPS**

METRICS FOR THE HUMAN FACTOR

by Jake Weatherly, Director of Customer Experience, Palo Alto Software

Performance Metrics—In the corporate world there is tremendous effort applied by management surrounding metrics, and this philosophy has trickled down to small business rapidly with affordable yet robust systems focused on metrics like CRM, IP phones, web analytics, search engine optimization, help desk ticketing and good old accounting. Why with all of this experience, infrastructure, and applied science is customer service generally terrible?

Key performance indicators in call centers surround call resolution time, call volume, number of open issues, and escalation data. Statistical analysis is done by another group of managers who are tasked with minimizing expenses and maximizing volume.

Even the smallest businesses are moving to outsourced call centers or building in-house teams based on these principals, and suddenly their unique competitive advantages—quality customer relationships, understanding goals and objectives, and domain expertise—are lost to real-time measurements that theoretically translate to higher levels of success. What is missing from these equations? If running successful call centers is such a science, why can't my small regional credit union implement my change of address after one request?

What are the *vital few* in customer satisfaction?

It all boils down to the human factor. Empathy, patience, and the true desire to help people are the foundation. Building skills surrounding these key factors to provide excellent service can be accomplished through training, experience and quality infrastructure.

The vital few of customer service are things like repeat business, size of initial purchase compared to subsequent purchases, and feedback, feedback, feedback!

Believe it or not feedback about how our software would be better if it did X, Y, or Z is a huge indication of customer satisfaction. This means that the customer is really using the

TIPS & TRAPS

METRICS FOR THE HUMAN FACTOR, CONTINUED

program, and they believe in the company behind the software enough to warrant taking time to share details about their experience.

When was the last time you sent the tech support person you spoke with a pizza for lunch? True story—we've received pizzas, unannounced visits, and even customers' plans to publish as thank you.

It does not get more measurable than a thank-you pizza from a customer!

That's in my vital few—I check on the number [of] thank-you pizzas we have received every day around noon.

Reprinted from *Business in General* with permission. All rights reserved.

- Some companies set an objective poll or survey, maybe even something as simple as what you can do at survey monkey.com, to measure intangibles like customer satisfaction.
- A software company might measure product quality by tracking support incidents or incidents by type. It might also measure the effectiveness of support providers by measuring minutes per call, or calls per incident, or by taking a survey of customers after their service transaction is finished.

I find that in general, developing the metrics required to bring your people into the planning process is very important. Get the people involved in how they are going to be measured. Often the team leaders fail to realize how well the players on the team know their specific functions and how they should be measured.

KEY NEW ENGLAND PATRIOTS STAT: RESTROOM WAIT TIME FOR WOMEN

How Analytics Help Build this Champion

Posted by Tom Davenport on January 31, 2008 8:54 A.M.

Last spring, on baseball's Opening Day, I confidently identified the Boston Red Sox on these very pages as the eventual World Series winner—based in part on their analytical prowess. You may recall that I was correct in that prediction. This Sunday, I will go out on a much more solid limb and pick the Patriots to triumph in the Super Bowl. I'm more of a baseball guy than a football nut, but fortunately both of the Boston teams I cheer for are not only winners of late, but also heavy users of analytical approaches to their respective games (the Celtics aren't doing badly either, but I think Kevin Garnett is more of a factor in their success than any statistician).

Like the Red Sox (or any analytically-oriented sports team, for that matter) the primary analytical application for the Pats is selecting the best players for the lowest price. This is particularly critical in the NFL, with its stringent salary cap. In-depth analytics helped the team select its players and conserve its dough. (Until last year the team had only a middle-ranking payroll in the National Football League, but now Tom Brady is getting expensive!) The team selects players using its own scouting services rather than the NFL-generic one that other teams employ; Brady, for example, was the 199th pick in 2000. They rate potential draft choices on such nontraditional factors as intelligence and willingness to subsume personal ego for the benefit of the team (though I had my doubts about their fidelity to that variable when they signed the famously mercurial Randy Moss before this season).

The Patriots also make extensive use of analytics for on-the-field decisions. They employ statistics, for example, to decide whether to punt or "go for it" on fourth down, whether to try for one point or two after a touchdown, and whether to throw out the yellow flag and challenge a referee's ruling. Both its coaches and players (particularly quarterback Tom

KEY NEW ENGLAND PATRIOTS STAT:
RESTROOM WAIT TIME FOR WOMEN, CONTINUED

Brady) are renowned for their extensive study of game video and statistics, and head coach Bill Belichick has been known to peruse articles by academic economists on statistical probabilities of football outcomes—over breakfast cereal, the legend goes.

Off the field, the team uses detailed analytics to assess and improve the "total fan experience." At every home game, for example, twenty to twenty-five people have specific assignments to make quantitative measurements of the stadium food, parking, personnel, bathroom cleanliness, and other factors. The team prides itself not only on scoring the most points ever this season, but also on having the lowest wait time for women's restrooms in the NFL. External vendors of services are monitored for contract renewal and have incentives to improve their performance. This won't help them win the Super Bowl, but it helps fill Gillette Stadium every home game.

Belichick deserves a lot of credit for the analytical emphasis (God knows, he can't get by on charm), but so do the team's owners. Just as the Red Sox owner John Henry moved the Sox in an analytical direction, Bob and (especially, I'm told) Jonathan Kraft believed that analytics could make a difference in football. Jonathan is a Harvard Business School alumnus and a former management consultant. In addition to Belichick, they hired Scott Pioli, a former Wall Street investment analyst and now the "player personnel" guru.

The only thing the Patriots lack is an analytical secret weapon equivalent to Bill James, the god of baseball statistics who acts as a "senior adviser" to the Sox. I'm not sure there is a Bill James of football. If there is, the Pats need to hire him (or her). Such a move could keep the Patriots dynasty going for many years to come.

From Harvard Business's discussionleader.hbsp.com, posted on January 31, 2008, discussionleader.hbsp.com/davenport/2008/01/how_analytics_help_build_this.html.

If you like trendy terms, the buzzword these days is *scorecard*. Business analysts use scorecard techniques to measure and track performance beyond the simple financial reports.

Milestones Make Your Business Plan a Real Plan

Use a milestones table to plan what's actually going to happen. I have provided a simple example in Figure 4.3. It's not much more than a list of what's supposed to happen, when it will start, when it will finish, what the budget is, who's in charge, and—in this example, at least—which department is responsible. To me it's the most important table in a business plan, because it's so obviously important for tracking progress and making your planning part of your management.

You don't need to get sophisticated with the milestones. A good list is enough.

Milestone	Start Date	End Date	Budget	Manager	Department
Corporate Identity	1-Dec	17-Dec	$10,000	TJ	Marketing
Seminar implementation	1-Jan	10-Jan	$1,000	IR	Sales
Business Plan Review	2-Jan	11-Jan	$0	RJ	GM
Upgrade mailer	2-Jan	17-Jan	$5,000	IR	Sales
New corporate brochure	2-Jan	17-Jan	$5,000	TJ	Marketing
Delivery vans	1-Jan	25-Jan	$12,500	SD	Service
Direct mail	2-Feb	17-Feb	$3,500	IR	Marketing
Advertising	2-Feb	17-Feb	$115,000	RJ	GM
X4 Prototype	1-Feb	25-Feb	$2,500	SG	Product
Service revamp	1-Feb	25-Feb	$2,500	SD	Product
6 Presentations	2-Feb	26-Feb	$0	IR	Sales
X4 Testing	1-Mar	6-Mar	$1,000	SG	Product
3 Accounts	1-Mar	17-Mar	$0	SD	Sales
L30 Prototype	1-Mar	26-Mar	$2,500	PR	Product
Tech Expo	1-Apr	12-Apr	$15,000	TB	Marketing
VP S&M hired	1-Jun	11-Jun	$1,000	JK	Sales
Mailing System	1-Jul	25-Jul	$5,000	SD	Service
Totals			$181,500		

Figure 4.3 **Sample Milestones Tables**

Using simple software (meaning Microsoft Excel, Apple iWork, Lotus 1-2-3, or of course, Business Plan Pro), you can sort the list by date, by manager, or by department, so you can, for example, use these milestones as agenda setters for the review meetings. Sort by manager to set the discussion points when you work with the people on your team to set expectations and follow up by reviewing results.

When and if you're thinking about plan document output, a set of milestones makes a good chart, like the one in Figure 4.4.

This is the bread and butter of real business planning. You can't build implementation unless you put it into meaningful steps. Then, of course, you have to follow up on it, make it happen. Management is *setting expectations and following up on results*.

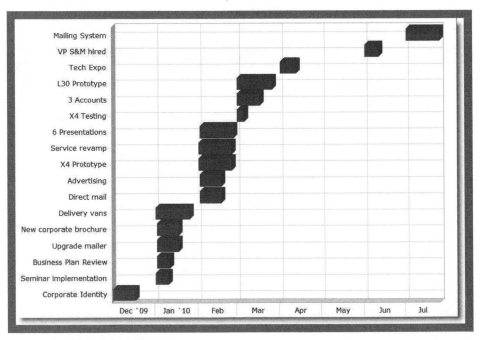

Figure 4.4 **Milestones Chart**

Strategy Pyramid

The strategy pyramid is a simple framework to help you think through the steps to take. The question is how to go from strategy to concrete and practical steps. I developed this idea and named it the strategy pyramid back in the mid-'80s. I was consulting with the Latin American group of Apple Computer, led by Hector Saldana. I had done the group's annual business plan for three years when Saldana issued a challenge: "We want you to manage our annual plan again this year, but with a difference. This year we want you to sit with us the rest of the year and make sure we actually implement it."

The repeat business for my consulting was good news, but there was a catch. The Apple Latin America group at that time was a collection of a couple dozen young, well-educated, brilliant people. Saldana and I were the only ones over 30 years old. It was hard to keep that group focused. Strategy takes boring consistency to implement. The strategy was desktop publishing, but we'd been working with that for so long that multimedia was much more interesting—to the managers, but not to the market (see Figure 4.5).

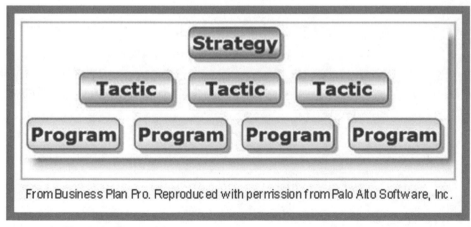

From Business Plan Pro. Reproduced with permission from Palo Alto Software, Inc.

Figure 4.5 **Strategy Pyramid**

So I came up with the strategy pyramid, which made it possible to track implementation and work on strategic alignment. We used it to build a database of business activities that we called programs and track them back up through tactics and strategy. One strategy, for example, was to emphasize desktop publishing. Tactics included advertising, pricing of bundles, and distribution channels. The detailed programs were things like advertising insertions, seminar marketing, bundling of hardware and software, and distributor pricing. Each program was assigned a manager, a start date, an end date, and a budget. Sometimes the budget was zero. The database incorporated an input spending amount for every activity, but that didn't involve spending. Leaving a zero was allowed.

The result was strategic alignment. The next year we were able to sort and manage programs according to strategies and tactics. We could show a spending pie divided into pieces representing each of our strategic priorities. We could also track implementation to the level of specific tasks assigned to specific managers, with performance on start date, finish date, and budget. In some cases we could even track sales back to projections in the plan. So seminar programs that began with sales projections had to live with sales results.

Focus on three or four main strategic priorities and build a conceptual pyramid for each one.

You can use the strategy pyramid in your own planning. Focus on three or four main strategic priorities and build a conceptual pyramid for each one. Don't sweat the details like definitions of strategies and tactics; just make it work for you, in your business, with your pyramid. Do sweat the details like making programs with specific responsibilities, budgets, and projected outputs when possible.

You don't have to be a big company. Apple was a huge company to me in the mid-'80s, because it had more than 1,000 employees; yet the Latin American group had fewer than two dozen people. We made the pyramid work because we wanted to make it work; we wanted to build strategy, not just great parties.

Remember, good business planning is nine parts implementation for every one part strategy.

Adapted from a column for Entrepreneur.com.

Value-Based Marketing

This is just a thought, a tip, not something you're supposed to do or have to do. But it might help. The idea of value-based marketing can help you figure out what to do to take your core strategy into specific activities to reach your customers.

1. It starts with what the experts call a *value proposition*. In its simplest forms that is benefit offered minus price charged. Price is relative. So an automaker might offer a more comfortable car at a price premium. Or a safer car or a faster car. A national fast-food chain probably offers the value of convenience and reliability, probably at a slight price premium (at least when compared with the weaker chains). A prestigious local restaurant, on the other hand, is offering a completely different set of benefits (luxury, elegance, prestige, for example) at a marked price premium. A graphic designer is probably selling benefits related to communication and advertising, not just drawings.

   Price is relative.

2. Then you communicate the value proposition to your customers. The restaurants communicate with customers using their location (drive-through facility, perhaps, or a playground for kids), their menu, and also decor (bright colors for one, fancy table dressings and white tablecloths for another) and signage and lots of other messages. What do you think about a mostly-crab restaurant that

plays loud music and has peanut shells covering the floor? And of course there's the more obvious advertising, collaterals, websites, and what employees say and do, and how they are dressed. For example, if a computer store's business proposition has to do with reliable service for small businesses, peace of mind, and long-term relationships, then it probably shouldn't be taking out full-page newspaper advertisements promising the lowest prices in town on brand-name hardware. It probably should communicate its proposition with sales literature that emphasizes how the computer store will become a strategic ally of its clients. It might also think twice about how it handles overdue bills from customers, who might really be holding out for more service or better support. Look at specific business activities.

3. None of this works if you don't deliver on the promise. The expensive restaurant needs to deliver good food well, with good service. The fast-food restaurant needs to deliver food quickly. The automaker claiming safety, speed, reliability, or whatever has to deliver on those claims.

Where all of this becomes particularly interesting is what when you do doesn't line up with what you say. Or what you promise isn't what you deliver. I worked with a computer store that promised reliability and peace of mind to small-business customers but didn't deliver until it finally revamped its business plan to include more service training, more installation, white delivery vans, and the promise not to cut prices to compete with every box-pushing office superstore.

And the value proposition should show up in all functional areas of the business, not just the sales pitch. For example, do the people who collect the bills know that you are trying to offer your customers superior service? How about the people who receive returns at the customer service counter?

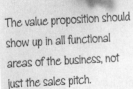

The value proposition should show up in all functional areas of the business, not just the sales pitch.

Value-based marketing should be included in the action plan, the activities, most of which are listed on the milestones table. It's a way to give some logic to the actual sales and marketing and administration and related everyday business activities.

All Those Ps

You have a marketing strategy. It's the heart of your plan. You've talked it out, probably written it out. You may have done the market research and industry research, or maybe you're just sure of yourself in your market. We used to call it the marketing mix, or the three Ps (pricing, promotion, and an artificially forced place to stand for distribution and make the alliteration work). Then it became fashionable to make it four Ps by adding product. And even five Ps, to include packaging.

Value-based marketing should be included in the action plan.

The problem, at this point, is knowing what to do, specifically with each of those Ps. That's the heart of the action plan.

One of the biggest problems many businesses face is strategic alignment. By that I mean making what you do every day match what you say is your strategy. It's amazing to me how often the daily activities don't match the strategy. That's why I've included the *strategy pyramid* and *value-based marketing* as part of this book. More than that, though, as you fill out the what's-supposed-to-happen parts of your plan-as-you-go plan, I hope you get turned on to new ways of marketing.

Being Remarkable

Marketing has changed. It's about being remarkable. Don't fill in your marketing plan until you've been through at least one of Seth Godin's books from the list in Figure 4.6. I don't know which to recommend most. *Purple Cow* is perhaps the best summary of a new kind of marketing, but *All Marketers Are Liars* is great reading and

**Purple Cow: Transform Your
Business by Being
Remarkable**
by Seth Godin

**Guerilla Marketing in 30
Days
(Guerrilla Marketing)**
by Levinson, Al Lautenslager

**Duct Tape Marketing: The
World's Most Practical Small
Business Marketing Guide**
by John Jantsch

**Meatball Sundae: Is Your
Marketing out of Sync?**
by Seth Godin

**All Marketers Are Liars: The
Power of Telling Authentic
Stories in a Low-Trust World**
by Seth Godin

Figure 4.6 **Essential
Reading about
Marketing**

makes its points in a more direct way. *Meatball Sundae* is the latest, released early in 2008.

John Jantsch's *Duct Tape Marketing* has transformed service marketing for small and medium companies. It's more method than approach. It's full of specific steps to take. And it's very much rooted in the new world of blogs and social media and Web 2.0.

Conrad Levinson and Al Lautenslager's *Guerilla Marketing in 30 Days* has had remarkable staying power for more than 20 years. It was written before the internet became widely available, but still managed to foresee a lot of what has happened since then. Levinson was probably the first to free marketing from the corporate budget.

What's still critical is the message and how to deliver it, to whom, and for how much money. It has to do with focusing on your key target market, figuring out the media, and getting that message across. Marketing is delightfully creative. What you want in your business plan at this point is something specific about what you're going to do and how much it's going to cost.

Aside from the target market strategy, your marketing strategy might also include the positioning statement, pricing, promotion, and whatever else you want to add. You might also want to look at media strategy, business development, or other factors. Strategy is creative and hard to predict. Some of the following sections will give you more ideas.

Positioning Still Matters

Positioning is an old-fashioned buzzword, but it still works. I talked about positioning earlier, while discussing the heart of the plan. The question is how do you do it? You can use advertising, marketing collaterals, your website, your employees, so many different methods. Try this positioning statement to help:

> *For [target market description] who [target market need], [this product] [how it meets the need]. Unlike [key competition], it [most important distinguishing feature].*

For example, the positioning statement for the original Business Plan Pro was "For the businessperson who is starting a new company, launching new products or seeking funding or partners, Business Plan Pro is software that produces professional business plans quickly and easily. Unlike [name omitted], Business Plan Pro does a real business plan, with real insights, not just cookie-cutter fill-in-the-blanks templates."

Pricing

One of the strongest messages you deliver is your price. It's also the most important tool for positioning. Don't

One of the strongest messages you deliver is your price.

be afraid to price at a premium if you're offering a premium product. In today's world, it isn't true that lower price necessarily delivers higher volume. That may be a standard of microeconomics, but it doesn't happen that often in the real world. Consider your value proposition. Does your pricing fit your strategy?

Promotion Means Telling Your Story

Promotion is a pompous word. I would call it telling your story or spreading the word. It isn't just what Seth Godin calls shouting, which he uses to refer to traditional advertising that interrupts people.

For a lot of today's businesses, it's very much a matter of website positioning and guessing about search terms to buy from Google. In retail, it's about location, signage, interior design, and the kind of positioning that has to do with what you sell and to whom, for what price.

For products going into distribution channels and eventually to retail, packaging is still critical. Consumers in stores make so many of their buying decisions based on packaging. Does the packaging support the underlying story? Do you have strategic alignment with the packaging? Does it match the rest of your positioning?

And, of course, you still have the old standbys for more traditional marketing.

- Do you look for expensive ads in mass media, or targeted marketing in specialized publications, or even more targeted messages with direct mail?
- Do you have a way to leverage the news media or reviewers?
- Do you advertise more effectively through public relations events, trade shows, newspaper, or radio?
- What about telemarketing, the web, or even multilevel marketing?

For products going into distribution channels and eventually to retail, packaging is still critical.

You Say Your Plan Every Day

Jim Blasingame, small business advocate, has a website at jbsba.com and an ask-the-expert site at askjim.biz. I'm on his radio talk show roughly once a month. As I was preparing this chapter, I was on the radio with Blasingame talking about it and he referred to his "Don't Be Intimidated" article, which he summarized as "You say your business plan every day."

In that newsletter article (which can be found at jbsba.com), Blasingame imagines the following conversation:

Me: Hi Joe. Heard you are starting a new business. What kind?

You: Oh, hi Jim. Thanks for asking. Yeah, John and I are going to be selling square widgets to round widget distributors.

Me: How're you going to do that?

You: I found out that no one has thought to offer square widgets to these guys. I asked around, and it looks like these guys not only NEED square widgets, but they will pay a premium for them.

Me: Sounds good. Where are you going to get your square widgets?

You: I found out that the round widget guys don't need the perfect square widgets, so I am buying seconds, cleaning them up a little, and repackaging them for my round widget customers.

Me: Sounds like you found a niche. How many can you sell in a year?

You: We've identified the need for 15,000 this year, and with the trend in the market, we think we can double that within three years. Gotta go. See you later.

How long did this conversation take—two minutes from start to end? Let's look at what was said. You identified your

- business;
- management team;
- industry;
- business focus (your niche);
- customer profile;
- vendor profile;
- pricing strategy;
- market research; and
- growth plans.

See? You probably "say" your business plan every day, you just might not be getting it down on paper, or in your computer.

This kind of core value is one of your business drivers. This is a lot of what I mean by the heart of the plan, the elevator speech. If you're normal, your interested in this, you think about it a lot, and you refine and revise it as necessary in a changing world, changing market. Build your business plan around this core, like leaves surrounding an artichoke's heart.

Basic Business Numbers

You may not have the need for a complete financial forecast, but it's just a shame to run a business without managing a simple sales forecast, expense budget, and—if and only if you're planning a startup—an estimate of startup costs. These are all relatively simple estimates, with relatively simple math that anybody who is smart enough to run a business can handle.

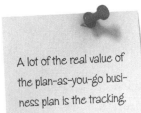

A lot of the real value of the plan-as-you-go business plan is the tracking.

After all, a lot of the real value of the plan-as-you-go business plan is the tracking, following up, seeing what was different between what actually happened and what was planned. That's much more likely to occur if you have numbers, like sales and expenses, that you can track.

Furthermore, you really should also be aware of the very important cash traps that can kill your business even if it's growing and profitable. These traps are avoidable.

TIPS & TRAPS

YES, YOU ARE QUALIFIED TO FORECAST YOUR BUSINESS

There's a scene in one of the Monty Python movies in which the woman on the operating table is about to give birth. Frightened, she asks the doctor—a memorable John Cleese character—"Doctor, doctor, what do I do?"

The doctor, looking down at her with a sneer, answers, "You? Nothing. You're not qualified!"

It's a very funny scene. I'm a man. I've been present for several births. I know who does everything. Not the doctor.

The same strange hesitance shows up a lot when people in business need to forecast. They think somebody else, somebody with more schooling, knows better. Someone else can run the numbers, do an econometric analysis, look at the data better, find the trends.

The truth, however, is that nobody is more qualified than a business owner to forecast her business. You've been there, you've lived through the ups and downs of it, you have the sense of it better than anybody.

For the record, I spent several years as a vice president in a brand-name market research consulting company. Our clients often thought we knew better, because that's how we made our living. And most of the time we were just making educated guesses, like you do when you forecast your own business.

You are qualified. Trust yourself.

So in this section what I want to get you into the basic numbers that can run your business. There is so much benefit from tracking the difference between sales forecasts and actual sales; this is where you really get into the planning process and managing your business better.

Don't worry, this isn't (yet) a full-blown financial forecast. Don't call your local accountant or management consultant. The math is simple, and although the educated guessing isn't, you can do it, and you are uniquely qualified. Here's what we're going to look at:

1. *A sales forecast.* How to do it, why to do it, what to look for, how much to do.
2. *Your spending budget.* You need to know—and track changes in—the money flowing out of your business. This is related to burn rate, fixed and variable costs, and milestones. It's real management. This ought to include just a few of the most important parts of spending:
   - costs of sales
   - a simple expense budget
   - starting costs (this is necessary only if you're planning a startup. If so, you will have expenses that will get deducted from future income, and you'll have assets that you'll have to buy. You want to have a good idea of what it will take to get started before you get halfway there.)
3. *Cash-flow traps.* Just so you know, we're going to leave the full-blown financial forecast, with its standard formats, balances, and accrual accounting and definitions and all, for the following chapter about dressing the plan as needed. But we can't pretend we have you in good shape with numbers if we aren't anticipating the cash-flow traps that can kill even profitable and growing businesses.

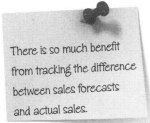

There is so much benefit from tracking the difference between sales forecasts and actual sales.

Forecasting Is More Art Than Science

Think of the weather forecast. You don't have to study the process to know what's going on. In the background, there's a community of meteorologists and public sector agencies gathering lots of data, constantly, on winds and clouds and pressure. The forecast takes that data into account and guesses the future, usually adding human judgment to the mix. For example, in the past, when things looked like this, it usually rained. So they call that a 70 percent chance of rain.

© Niels Lan, Jose Antonio, Santiso Fernández/iStock photo

Do you think every weather forecast requires some defined amount of data processing? Or, to ask that question another way, do you ever look at the horizon and see clouds looming or rain in the hills and predict, accurately, that it's going to rain where you are? Of course you do.

Here's an interesting statistic: in Palo Alto, California, if you predicted today's weather by saying, "It wil be the same as yesterday," you'd be right more than 75 percent of the days in a normal year.

Sometimes almost everybody knows the weather by looking at the sky. Sometimes only the data-rich people know the weather because what's coming shows up in the data—radar, pressures, wind speeds, storms off shore, and so on—but not in the sky.

Now take this idea to business forecasting. I think you have to get used to the idea that business forecasting, like weather forecasting, is a combination of data gathering and guessing. You want to have as much data as possible before you make an educated guess, because those guesses should be educated.

- You use past results of your own company first—if you have a company and you have past results—and think through how and why future results might be different.
- Whether you have past results, you use available industry averages as well. Find out about sales per employee or sales per square foot for your industry. Or use the reverse telephone tree (see sidebar) to get help from people with more industry experience. Look at financial reports published by the publicly traded companies in your industry, because they are required by law to report details.

THE TELEPHONE TREE IN REVERSE

So you want to know something you don't know. Here's one way to find out.

Get on the phone. Think of somebody to call first. Come on, you can think of somebody. Somebody who might have some idea. No ideas at all? Then call up the local small business development center if you have one near you, or the equivalent development agency if you're not in the United States. Or call a local bank and ask for somebody who works with business loans. Call the nearest business school. Call your cousin who owns her own business. Call somebody.

Unless you're really lucky, that first person won't have the answers you need. Don't worry. Ask her whom she knows who might have the answer.

Every person you call, ask who else might know.

Eventually, you'll find out as much as you're going to. It's not magic. You don't get to know everything about every subject. Particularly with business planning, sometimes you have to guess.

And remember as you forecast that it's just the first step. You're not going to live with your forecast for that long, because (at least with the plan-as-you-go business plan) you'll be reviewing and revising as soon as you get results.

Forecast Your Sales

Your sales forecast is the backbone of your business plan. People measure a business and its growth by sales, and your sales forecast sets the standard for expenses, profits, and growth. The sales forecast is almost always going to be the first set of numbers you'll track for plan vs. actual use. This is what you'll do even if you do no other numbers.

When it comes to forecasting sales, don't fall for the trap that says forecasting takes training, mathematics, or advanced degrees. Forecasting is mainly educated guessing. So don't expect to get it perfect; just make it reasonable. There's no business owner who isn't qualified to forecast sales—you don't need a business degree or accountant's certification. What you need is common sense, research of the factors, and motivation to make an educated guess.

Forecasting is mainly educated guessing.

Your sales forecast in a business plan should show sales by month for the next 12 months—at least—and then by year for the following two to five years. Three years, total, is generally enough for most business plans.

If you have more than one line of sales, show each line separately and then add them up. If you have more than ten or so lines of sales, summarize them and consolidate. Remember, this is business planning, not accounting, so *it* has to be reasonable, but it doesn't need too much detail. Figure 4.7 is an example from a sales forecast for a local computer retail store.

Sales Forecast	Jan	Dec	Year1	Year 2
Unit Sales				
Systems	85	275	2,255	2,500
Service	200	343	3,128	6,000
Software	150	490	3,980	5,000
Training	145	200	2,230	4,000
Other	160	200	2,122	2,500
Total Unit Sales	740	1,508	13,715	20,000
Unit Prices	Jan	Dec	Year 1	Year 2
Systems	$2,000.00	$1,984.50	$1,980.80	$1,984.50
Service	$75.00	$67.00	$68.54	$84.00
Software	$200.00	$207.00	$212.87	$195.00
Training	$37.00	$50.00	$46.54	$72.00
Other	$300.00	$300.00	$394.21	$300.00
Sales				
Systems	$170,000	$545,736	$4,466,708	$4,961,240
Service	$15,000	$22,981	$214,388	$504,000
Software	$30,000	$101,430	$847,220	$975,000
Training	$5,365	$10,000	$103,795	$288,000
Other	$48,000	$60,000	$836,520	$750,000
Total Sales	$268,365	$740,147	$6,468,631	$7,478,240

Figure 4.7 **Sales Forecast for a Computer Retail Store**

It's a simple example. You should recognize the arrangement of rows and columns. I'm just showing you a portion of the spreadsheet, because it has to fit on the page.

Notice the predictable structure. First you have units, then prices, then you multiply price times units to get sales. It's simple math, but breaking it up like that makes things easier later on, when you want to look at what went wrong (and remember, something will go wrong; business plans are always wrong).

Even if you've never done a spreadsheet, you can do this one. The hard part is remembering that you can estimate, you are qualified, and nobody else can do it better. Just take a deep breath, calm down, and make an estimate.

SNAPSHOTS OF SPREADSHEETS

Just a quick note. I hope it's obvious. With the examples in this book I'm not showing you the full columns of the spreadsheets, because that would be awkward. Numbers would be very small and difficult to read. I use my spreadsheets for sales forecasting and other normal monthly projections with a standard layout.

I base my tables on the standard spreadsheet layout as used in Microsoft Excel, Lotus 1-2-3, AppleWorks, Quattro Pro, and even the true pioneer, VisiCalc, the first spreadsheet software, from 30 years ago. The rows are labeled from 1 to whatever, and the columns are labeled from A to whatever. When you get past the 26 letters of the alphabet you start over again, with AA, AB, AC, and so on.

Labels in Column A	Special uses for Column B	12 Months Monthly in Columns C–N	Annual Columns as Needed
I run the labels along the lefthand side. These might be Sales, Expenses, Profits, etc.	I keep Column B open for variables like growth rates and such. This is convenient for starting balances too.	My months go off toward the right, one by one, in 12 columns.	The first year's totals of the numbers from the previous 12 months. Then come the additional years as needed.

Or, if you prefer, read on. Let's talk about working from past data, estimating entirely new products, your data analysis qualifications, and some other factors. Then you can make your forecast.

TIPS & TRAPS

SPREADSHEET BASICS

You probably know this already, but I'll go over it just in case. I recommend using Business Plan Pro software so you don't have to do this, but it's good to know anyhow, and you can certainly do everything in this book without that software. So here's a bit about spreadsheets.

Spreadsheets are normally arranged in rows and columns, with rows numbered from 1 to whatever, and columns labeled from A to whatever. Simple mathematical formulas refer to the cells that are identified by row and column. For example:

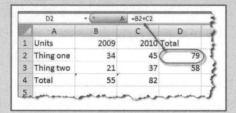

So what we see here is a simple formula that adds the 34 in cell B2 to the 45 in cell C2 to get the sum of those two, which is 79. That number is in cell D2, so you see the formula showing at the top when you click on D2. Also the number in the upper left corner indicates which cell the displayed formula belongs to.

Here's another simple example:

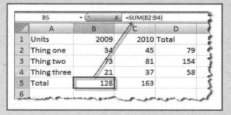

In this case the cell named B5 is highlighted, and its formula says to sum up all the cells from B2 to B4. That's three cells, and the numbers they contain sum up to 128.

There are lots of books and websites and different instructions and tutorials available for spreadsheets. This is enough for now, so you can understand my simple forecast examples.

Sometimes Timing Matters a Whole Lot

Don't reinvent wheels. Please. As you do your sales forecast, be aware that accountants and financial analysts have definite meanings for timing of sales. If you don't deal with this their way, then when you do eventually incorporate the work you've already done on the sales forecast into more formal financial projections, you'll have it wrong. It will look bad.

Timing of Sales

Your sales are supposed to refer to when the ownership changes hands (for products) or when the service is performed (for services). It isn't a sale when it is ordered, or promised, or even when it's contracted. With proper accrual accounting, it is a sale even if it hasn't been paid for. With so-called cash-based accounting, by the way, it isn't a sale until it's paid for. Accrual is better because it gives you a more accurate picture, unless you're very small and do all your business, both buying and selling, with cash only.

I know that seems simple, but it's surprising how many people decide to do something different. And the penalty of doing things differently is that then you don't match the standard, and the bankers, analysts, and investors can't tell what your numbers mean.

It isn't a sale when it is ordered, or promised, or even when it's contracted.

Timing of Costs

Costs of sales or direct costs or costs of goods sold are supposed to be timed to match the sale.

For example, when you buy a book from a bookstore, whatever that book cost the store to purchase was an amount added to inventory until you purchased it, and only then, with the purchase, it became an amount added to cost of goods sold.

Notice the timing. It sits in inventory for as long as it takes, but it doesn't get out of inventory and turn into cost of sales until it gets sold.

SO WHAT'S ACCRUAL ACCOUNTING AND WHY DOES IT MATTER?

Say you make a sale. When you deliver the goods, you record it as a sale. If the customer doesn't pay you immediately, you record the *accrued* amount as accounts receivable.

Then you order some goods. When you receive them, you don't pay for them. Instead, you record the *accrued* amount as accounts payable.

At the end of the tax year you have some expenses outstanding, like professional services you know you'll be billed for in the future. You *accrue* those expenses into the current tax year. They are deductible against income.

In so-called *cash basis* accounting, the opposite of accrual accounting, you don't put the sale or the purchase onto your books until the money changes hands. With business-to-business sales, the norm is that the money changes hands later. So *accrual accounting* is better. It gives your books a more accurate picture of your financial flow and financial position.

Why does this matter here? Because timing of sales, costs, and expenses makes a difference. Start your forecasts correctly so they can be part of a more formal financial forecast when you finally need one.

Messing that up can mess up your financial projections. When sales for the month are $25,000 and costs of goods sold are $10,000, you want the $10,000 to be the costs it took to buy whatever was sold for $25,000. If this month's costs are for things sold last month, or things sold next month, you get bad information.

It's harder to keep track of this sometimes with services. The cost of sales for a taxi ride should be the gas, the maintenance, and the driver's compensation. But accountants would go crazy trying to match the exact gasoline costs to the exact trip, so they estimate a lot. They are always trying to match the months, though; costs should be recorded in the same months as the corresponding sales.

Timing of Expenses

Expenses are supposed to show up in the month that they happen. Ideally, travel expenses are attributed to the month in which you travel, even if you paid the airfare two months earlier. Ideally, advertising expenses are recorded for the month when the ad appears in print, rather than the month when you submitted the ad. And they certainly should not appear in the month in which you pay for the ad, which often is two or three months later. You want the timing to match.

How Could I Know?

One of the more powerful drags on business planning in general is what I call fear of forecasting. Lots of people have it.

"How could I possibly know?" is one of the more popular complaints. After all, who can predict the future? How can you know what's going to happen in the market, with the competition, or with new technologies? Isn't it just wasting your time to try to guess?

> One of the more powerful drags on business planning in general is what I call fear of forecasting.

No, it isn't just wasting your time, because one thing harder to do than forecasting is running a company without a forecast. The real question isn't, How can I possibly know what's going to happen? but rather, How can I possibly know whether what actually does happen is good or bad or better than expected if I don't know what I thought would happen?

Confusing? Think of it this way: although you forecast for at least a year, you actually go out on a limb only for the next month. In a month, you're going to review that forecast. You're going to see what is different from the forecast and revise the forecast. Your year doesn't stay static after the first month if results of the first month cast doubt on the whole year.

So don't worry so much; get started with your forecast, and you'll be revising.

Example: Initial Sales Forecast for a Restaurant

Remember, there is no single way to forecast any business. It's often a very creative process.

Magda was looking at forecasting sales for a small restaurant. She hadn't locked in the location at that point, but she had a pretty good idea of the small size she wanted. She decided she would be able to seat six tables of four people each as a starting point. She knew that things might change when she actually decided on the space to rent, but she had to start somewhere, so six tables of four it was.

Then she did some simple math: six tables of four meant at capacity she would be serving 24 meals. Meals take about an hour at lunch and about two hours at dinner. She figured she'd have one serving of lunch and two of dinner, roughly calculating the 5 to 5:30 crowd as the first serving and the 7:30 to 8:00 crowd as the second serving. So an absolutely full lunch service in a day would be 24 lunches. An absolutely full dinner service in a day would be 48 dinners.

She decided that an average lunch would be $10 of food and $2 of beverages. And an average dinner would be $20 of food and $4 of beverages.

Now let's stop for a second to consider this. Magda isn't turning to some magic information source to find out what her sales will be. She isn't using quadratic equations and she doesn't need an advanced degree in calculus. She does need to have some sense of what to realistically expect. Ideally she's worked in a restaurant or knows somebody who has, so she has some reasonable information to draw on.

So, Magda can do a simple calculation to figure a good day's sales, when she is running at full capacity (see Figure 4.8):

1. Lunches are 24 x 10 + 24 x 2, which equals $288.
2. Dinners are 48 x 20 + 48 x 4, which equals $1,152.

	A	B	C	D	E	F	G	H	I	J	K
1	Developing Capacity										
2	Tables			6							
3	Seats per table			4							
4	Meals at capacity per serving			24							
5	Servings										
6		Lunches		1							
7		Dinners		2							
8	Beverages at capacity										
9		Lunches		1							
10		Dinners		2							
11	Calculated units at capacity										
12		Lunches		24							
13		Lunch Beverage		24							
14		Dinner		48							
15		Dinner Beverage		48							
16											
17											
18	Hypothetical average week										
19	Units	Capacity	Sun	Mon	Tues	Wed	Thurs	Fri	Sat	Total	Baseline month
20	Lunch	24	0	14	16	18	18	20	0	86	373
21	lunch beverage	24	0	14	16	18	18	20	0	86	373
22	Dinner	48	35	22	28	30	30	48	48	241	1,044
23	Dinner beverage	48	35	22	28	30	30	48	48	241	1,044
24	Total	144	70	72	88	96	96	136	96	654	2,834
25	Unit prices										
26	Lunch		$10.00	$10.00	$10.00	$10.00	$10.00	$10.00	$10.00		
27	lunch beverage		$2.00	$2.00	$2.00	$2.00	$2.00	$2.00	$2.00		
28	Dinner		$20.00	$20.00	$20.00	$20.00	$20.00	$20.00	$20.00		
29	Dinner beverage		$4.00	$4.00	$4.00	$4.00	$4.00	$4.00	$4.00		
30	Sales										
31	Lunch		$0	$140	$160	$180	$180	$200	$0	$860	$3,727
32	lunch beverage		$0	$28	$32	$36	$36	$40	$0	$172	$745
33	Dinner		$700	$440	$560	$600	$600	$960	$960	$4,820	$20,887
34	Dinner beverage		$140	$88	$112	$120	$120	$192	$192	$964	$4,177
35	Total		$840	$696	$864	$936	$936	$1,392	$1,152	$6,816	$29,536

Figure 4.8 **Sales Forecast for Magda's Restaurant**

Having figured out what sales might be in a maximum day, Magda looks at how sales might vary for the days of the week (see the second table in Figure 4.8). That provides a weekly baseline. It isn't just four weeks per month; multiply an average week times 52, then divide that product by 12 to get an average month. In the example, you can see how Magda estimated conservatively, with fewer dinners on Monday, and closing at lunch on Saturday and Sunday. She knows she's not going to get a full-capacity day that often. So she's calculated a baseline month, with around 370 lunches and 1,044 dinners. But she's also just starting up, so she came up with an educated guess for a lot lower than that, around half the capacity.

These numbers are not magic. The point of this example is simply that Magda has to find a way to make sense of her forecast. As you work with yours, don't look for some answer out there in the world, like a right answer to a puzzle; look for ways to break your assumptions down into the logic you need to work with them.

Magda should get on a computer and put her forecast in a spreadsheet. She can make four rows labeled Lunches, Lunch Beverages, Dinners, and Dinner Beverages. She should also add a row for Other, because there are always miscellaneous sales. Then she can spread these assumptions out with the simple math so she can see them on a month-by-month basis. (See Figure 4.9 for an example.)

If you don't know how to work a spreadsheet, using formulas for rows and columns, read the sidebar "Spreadsheet Basics" on page 134. Don't fear the math or the financing.

By the way, you can represent your forecast graphically, with the right tools. You might draw the line to help yourself visualize the way the numbers flow. Figure 4.10 is an example of how a simple line graph can forecast Magda's lunch sales for the first year.

Remember, please, these are not scientific numbers. They are based on assumptions. Magda will review these numbers every month and tune them against reality. So therefore she doesn't have

You can represent your forecast graphically, with the right tools.

	A	C	D	E
	B16			
16	**Sales Forecast**			
17		Jan	Feb	Mar
18	**Unit Sales**			
19	Lunches	119	227	302
20	Lunch Bvg	119	227	302
21	Dinners	500	600	728
22	Dinner Bvg	500	600	728
23	Other	50	50	50
24	**Total Unit Sales**	1,288	1,704	2,110
25				
26	**Unit Prices**	Jan	Feb	Mar
27	Lunches	$10.00	$10.00	$10.00
28	Lunch Bvg	$2.00	$2.00	$2.00
29	Dinners	$20.00	$20.00	$20.00
30	Dinner Bvg	$4.00	$4.00	$4.00
31	Other	$2.00	$2.00	$2.00
32				
33	**Sales**			
34	Lunches	$1,192	$2,272	$3,021
35	Lunch Bvg	$238	$454	$604
36	Dinners	$10,000	$12,000	$14,560
37	Dinner Bvg	$2,000	$2,400	$2,912
38	Other	$100	$100	$100
39	**Total Sales**	$13,530	$17,227	$21,197

Figure 4.9 **Monthly Sales Forecast for Magda's Restaurant**

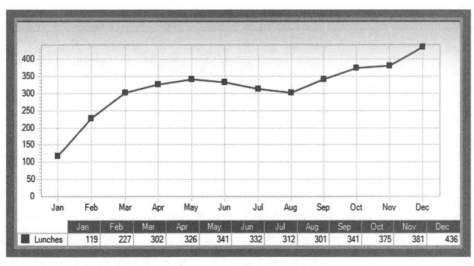

	Jan	Feb	Mar	Apr	May	Jun	Jul	Aug	Sep	Oct	Nov	Dec
■ Lunches	119	227	302	326	341	332	312	301	341	375	381	436

Figure 4.10 **Graph of Magda's Lunch Sales Forecast**

to guess right for long stretches into the future; she just has to start with a reasonable guess and then start tracking.

Furthermore, you don't have to be right from the beginning because as your business goes on, you constantly improve your forecast. After the first month, as you look at the second month and all the rest of the forecast, you have the results from the first month to work with. Always review, and revise as the review indicates.

Let's say that when Magda's first-month results come in, lunch sales are much lower than she thought, but dinner sales are slightly higher. See Figure 4.11.

Figure 4.12 shows the difference between what was planned and what happened.

	A	CP
16	**Actual Sales**	
17		Jan
18	**Unit Sales**	
19	Lunches	72
20	Lunch Bvg	124
21	Dinners	537
22	Dinner Bvg	323
23	Other	68
24	**Total Unit Sales**	1,124
25		
26	**Unit Prices**	Jan
27	Lunches	$11.90
28	Lunch Bvg	$2.59
29	Dinners	$19.85
30	Dinner Bvg	$7.17
31	Other	$1.21
32		
33	**Sales**	
34	Lunches	$857
35	Lunch Bvg	$321
36	Dinners	$10,657
37	Dinner Bvg	$2,316
38	Other	$82
39	**Total Sales**	$14,233

Figure 4.11 **Magda's Actual Sales for January**

DQ39	=SUM(DQ34:DQ38)	
	A	DI
16	**Sales Forecast**	
17		Jan
18	**Unit Sales**	
19	Lunches	(47)
20	Lunch Bvg	5
21	Dinners	37
22	Dinner Bvg	(177)
23	Other	18
24	**Total Unit Sales**	(164)
25		
26	**Unit Prices**	Jan
27	Lunches	$1.90
28	Lunch Bvg	$0.59
29	Dinners	($0.15)
30	Dinner Bvg	$3.17
31	Other	($0.79)
32		
33	**Sales**	
34	Lunches	($335)
35	Lunch Bvg	$83
36	Dinners	$657
37	Dinner Bvg	$316
38	Other	($18)
39	**Total Sales**	$703

Figure 4.12 **Difference between Forecasted Sales and Actual Sales for January**

Using these numbers, Magda revises her sales forecast for the rest of the years. Why wait? She had a logical first guess based on some simple numbers, but now she has real-world results. See Figure 4.13.

And now her sales forecast is up and running. Plan as you go.

More Sales Forecast Examples: Building the Numbers

Although we probably agree that the best way to forecast sales is by looking at past experience, I know that you can't always count on having that kind of information available to you. So let's think about some other examples. It's never as exact as it sounds. There's a lot of creative guessing. Following are a few ways you might forecast sales for a new business. The point isn't to list the only acceptable methods, but rather to suggest that anything logical might work.

A	C	D	E
16 Sales Forecast			
17	Jan	Feb	Mar
18 Unit Sales			
19 Lunches	72	90	150
20 Lunch Bvg	124	160	250
21 Dinners	537	700	825
22 Dinner Bvg	323	500	600
23 Other	68	40	50
24 **Total Unit Sales**	1,124	1,490	1,875
25			
26 Unit Prices	Jan	Feb	Mar
27 Lunches	$11.90	$12.00	$12.00
28 Lunch Bvg	$2.59	$2.75	$2.75
29 Dinners	$19.85	$20.00	$20.00
30 Dinner Bvg	$7.17	$7.00	$7.00
31 Other	$1.21	$1.25	$1.25
32			
33 Sales			
34 Lunches	$857	$1,080	$1,800
35 Lunch Bvg	$321	$440	$688
36 Dinners	$10,657	$14,000	$16,500
37 Dinner Bvg	$2,316	$3,500	$4,200
38 Other	$82	$50	$63
39 **Total Sales**	$14,233	$19,070	$23,250

Figure 4.13 **Magda's Revised Sales Forecast**

- *You want to sell products over your website?* OK, find a way to predict traffic. Maybe you can buy search terms. For example, with Google advertising, Google AdWords can help you estimate how many will see the link you buy for the search terms. Then you estimate how many of those people actually click your link. Estimate a very low percentage, less than 1 percent, unless you have the world's most compelling link. Then estimate how many of those actually buy what you're selling. That's a low percentage too. At least with this you've got some mathematical basis for unit sales. And if you're estimating more than one per thousand, be careful—it's probably too high.
- *Doing retail business?* Find some estimates of sales per square foot for your type of business. You can do a web search for

that, and you might find something useful. I found annual sales per square foot for Best Buy, Apple, Neiman Marcus, and Tiffany, and learned that Apple does $4,000 per square foot, compared with $2,600 for Tiffany and less than $1,000 for tho other two.

■ *Let's say you've self-published a book you wrote and paid to have the book printed.* Forecast your sales through different channels: Amazon.com and competing websites first, then perhaps through distributors to physical bookstores. But can you get that book into distribution? Will bookstores accept you? Use the reverse tree method and call other authors from the same print to see how they did. Do a web search on self-publishing. Start a blog and use search-term advertising to generate readers. Estimate how many people who visit your blog will click a link on it to buy your book. Build your sales forecast according to the places where people can buy the book: online at your site, online at other sites, and physically in stores. Be realistic about how long it takes to get into stores.

■ *You are opening up a bicycle store in a summer tourist destination.* Find an estimate of tourists, then estimate what percent end up renting a bike, then how many units that means, and go from there. Or count bike rentals per day and build up a forecast from there.

■ *Selling products through channels of distribution?* Maybe estimate unit sales by channels.

■ *During professional consulting?* Estimate by the job, the day, or the hour. Make assumptions based on leads.

■ *Lots of companies use pipeline analysis:* how many leads per marketing effort, how many presentations per lead, how many closes per presentation.

Whatever your business is, find some numbers and logic for it. Break your assumptions down into units, and price per unit, and make sure there's some way you can check on the logic and revise and track as the numbers flow in. The key to this is watching the actual results.

If You Can, Start from Last Year

If you can, whenever you can, start this year's forecast by putting last year's numbers onto this year's spreadsheet. Then revise as needed. One of the real luxuries of the existing and ongoing company, compared with the startup, is that there is data. You have experience.

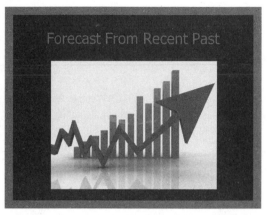

© Yártan Nersisian/iStock photo

As soon as you have a forecast with last year's numbers in it, start thinking about what's going to be different.

- What's new and different this year compared with last year? New products? New business relationships, new channels, new locations maybe?
- What about bad news? Sometimes things are cooling off, some new problems are developing. Maybe new competition shows up.
- Will pricing change?

You can look at costs and expenses, too. Normally we assume costs and expenses will rise gradually. That's just a general matter of inflation. Is it going to apply for your business in the next year? Why? Or why not?

If You Have a New Product

"But I have a new product; how can I forecast for that? There's no history."

Join the club. Lots of people start new businesses, or new groups or divisions or products or territories within existing businesses, and can't turn to existing data to use for forecasting the future.

You're still going to forecast, and don't worry so much about it, because although you'll do if for the next 12 months, you're going to be grossly inaccurate only for the first month. By the second month, you'll have data to use to revise your forecast.

Think of journalists covering a free election. They don't want to wait for the official results to be published, so they ask people coming out of polling places how they voted. Maybe those people tell the truth, and maybe not, but there's information to be gathered. They call these exit polls. And if the exit polls surprise people—they thought Jones was going to win by a landslide but the exit polls indicate Smith is winning—then the reporters investigate further. Are these early results coming from just one kind of voter (rich, poor, rural, urban, early voter, whatever), and does that one kind of voter favor Smith more than the rest of the voters? Time to apply common sense.

Business charts are excellent tools for understanding and estimating numbers.

You can do the same thing with your forecast that journalists do with elections. You can get what data is available and apply common sense to it, human judgment, and then make your educated guesses. As more information becomes available—like the first month's sales, for example—then you add that into the mix, and revise or not, depending on how well it matches your expectations.

It's not a one-time forecast that you have to live with as the months go by. It's all part of the plan-as-you-go process.

Graphics as Forecasting Tools

Business charts are excellent tools for understanding and estimating numbers. Use them to evaluate the projected numbers. When you view your forecast on a business chart, does it look real? Does it make sense? It turns out that most humans sense the relative size

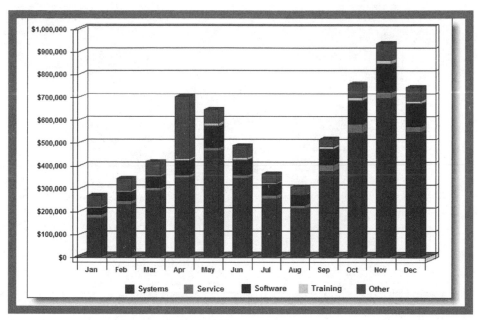

Figure 4.14 **Monthly Sales Forecast Chart**

of shapes better than they sense numbers, so we see a sales forecast differently when it's represented in a chart. Use the power of the computer to help you visualize your numbers.

For example, consider the monthly sales forecast chart in Figure 4.14. You can look at this chart and immediately see the ebbs and flows of sales during the year. Sales go up from January into April, then down from spring into summer, then up again beginning in September. When you look at a chart like that, you should ask yourself whether that pattern is correct. Is that the way your sales go?

The chart in Figure 4.15 shows a comparison of forecasted sales for three years. Here again you can sense the relative size of the numbers in the chart. If you knew the company involved, you'd be able to evaluate and discuss this sales forecast just by looking at the

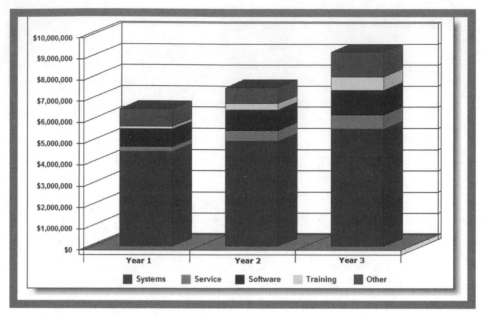

Figure 4.15 **Annual Sales Forecast Chart**

chart. Of course you'd probably want to know more detail about the assumptions behind the forecast, but you'd have a very good initial sense of the numbers.

When we did the *sample restaurant sales forecast*, we used a line graph to estimate the seasonality for the restaurant (see Figure 4.10).

Understanding Fixed and Variable Costs and Burn Rate

Costs are among the financial and accounting terms that have specific meanings. You can't just decide to think of them as what makes sense to you, because the accountants and analysts won't understand you. They'll say you are wrong. Ouch. Not pleasant.

So, here are some definitions.

Cost of Sales

The cost of sales is not the expenses related to making a sale. It isn't that lunch with the customer or the trip to go visit the customer and make a pitch. Cost of sales means what it costs you to make or deliver whatever it is you sell. If you don't sell, you don't have any costs. The costs are variable by definition.

- ■ *Costs are supposed to be directly related to sales.* They are about what it costs you to have or build or deliver what you're selling.
  - Costs of a manufactured product include materials and labor. So, for example, the computer costs $200 to build, including $150 in parts and $50 in labor.
  - If you just buy an already-built computer and then sell it, the cost is what you paid to buy it.
  - If you deliver a service, you still have costs. The taxi or airline has fuel, maintenance, and personnel costs. The law firm has what it pays the lawyers, plus legal assistants, and photocopying and research.
- ■ *Costs depend on who and when.* For example:
  - When you buy a book for $19.95 at the local bookstore, the store's cost of goods sold are whatever it paid to buy that book from the distributor. Let's say it paid $10.50 plus shipping. The store's sales are $19.95 and its cost of goods sold is $10.50 plus shipping.
  - If the distributor bought the book from the publisher for $6.25, then its sales for the book are $10.50, and its cost of goods sold is $6.25.
  - Let's say the publisher had the book printed for $2 per copy and it pays the author a royalty of 10 percent. Its sales for the book are $6.25 and its cost of goods sold is $2 plus $0.652 for royalty. And the publisher probably paid to ship the book to the distributor, which would add another small amount, maybe $0.25, to the cost of goods sold.
- ■ *Understand inventory.* This comes up again as a cash-flow trap.

- Stuff that's going to become cost of goods sold when it sells starts out as inventory, which is an asset. It sits there in inventory until it sells.
- Think about this in terms of timing and cash flow. The publisher buys the books from the printer and pays for them, which makes them inventory. They sit there for months until the distributor buys them, at which point they become cost of sales. The distributor has them as inventory until it sells them to the store. Then they become cost of sales. The store has the book for as long as it takes, from when it receives it and puts it on the shelf until you buy it.
- The cash-flow trap is that the whole inventory asset doesn't show up on your income statement until you sell the stuff. In the meantime, whether you've paid for it or not, the income statement doesn't care. The money is gone, but the sale hasn't been made. This is a classic cash-flow trap. You won't see it on the income statements. It is completely outside of the realm of profit and loss. But you have spent the money.

Here's where you rate yourself. If these ideas are obvious, then skip this next part; don't worry about it. If you're uncomfortable with these terms, vaguely worried you don't know what they mean, then read on, and in about five minutes, you will.

Fixed vs. Variable Costs

Part One: The Real Case—Manufacturing Costs

Sometimes this matters, many times it doesn't. Technically, fixed costs are costs that you pay regardless of whether or not you sell anything or how much you sell. For example, the monthly rental of an installation used exclusively to build stuff would be a fixed cost. It gets technical and surprisingly creative as cost accountants figure out how to allocate fixed costs to the related sales. That was a special course in business school. I found it fascinating, but for business planning purposes, let it go.

We're doing planning, not accounting. Remember?

Part Two: Fixed vs. Variable Costs and Risk

Don't worry too much about financial definitions, because in this case at least, they are inherently confusing. Analysts tend to talk about fixed vs. variable costs, but most of the time they are talking about variable costs (as in cost of sales, direct cost of goods, costs of goods sold) vs. fixed expenses (such as payroll and rent.) This is not a useful context for distinguishing between costs and expenses. Basically this is about trying to figure out how much risk you have in the business. And since fixed costs get paid whether you have sales to offset them, and variable costs happen only when you have sales, the higher the fixed costs, the more risk in the business.

Don't worry too much about financial definitions, because in this case at least, they are inherently confusing.

The big picture is relatively straightforward. The underlying assumption is that your spending has two parts: the fixed part, which you spend no matter what, and the variable part, which you spend only if you make the sale, and for which the level of spending depends (hence the term *variable*) entirely on the level of sales.

For an example of that, here's a true story. Back in the formative years of Palo Alto Software, we chose to pay an outside sales representation company 6 percent of our retail sales, after the fact, rather than hire somebody as an employee to manage retail sales.

The trade-off should be obvious. There was a lot less risk with the variable cost. If we didn't get the sale, we paid nothing. If we did get the sale, then we had money from the sale that we could use to pay the variable cost.

Some of your spending is almost always fixed: rent, insurance, payroll, for example. Some of your spending is almost always variable: direct cost of sales, for example.

And some of your spending is hard to classify. The plumber pays for the Yellow Pages advertisement in the telephone book once a year, regardless of sales levels, but if sales go up because of the ad, she might be tempted to increase the ad size next year. Your website seems like a fixed cost, but many of us in the web business pay commissions to affiliated sites that help us make sales.

It's fine-tuning like this that has given us the term *burn rate*. This concept became popular during the dotcom boom in the late 1990s. Some internet companies that had no sales or revenue had lots of money from investors. So they would divide the money they had in the bank by their monthly burn rate (how much money they were spending every month) to calculate how many months of life they had. Without sales or revenue, burn rate became very important. They'd use it to know when to look for more investment, or, in some cases, when to look for a new job. *Burn Rate*, by Michael Wolff, is a very entertaining book about it. You counted your future as how many months' worth of burn rate you had in the bank, from the investors.

I like using the term *burn rate* instead of *fixed costs*. Technically, fixed costs are costs that would stop if you didn't sell. But the burn rate, on the other hand, is how much money you spend every month, without quibbling over whether it's technically fixed costs or not. They are closely related.

All of this becomes more than just idle debate and definitions if you try to do a break-even analysis. I think of a break-even as mostly optional, but it's still a good illustration of your basic financial picture. So you might find it worth the effort for a break-even analysis tool. Look in the business calculators section of bplans.com. There's also a detailed break-even explanation at hurdlebook.com.

Your Burn Rate

Your burn rate is how much you have to spend on an average month to keep your company up and running. That normally includes rent, payroll, and—unlike the concepts of fixed and variable costs—whatever else you spend in a normal month that isn't directly tied to your sales, which means it isn't automatically paid for by sales, whether it's fixed or variable. So it includes your standard marketing expenses, which would technically be called variable expenses.

I think you should always know your burn rate. I hope you have sales and revenue as well. If your plan calls for burning more money than you're bringing in, then you know you need to be borrowing or finding investment capital.

I also like the burn rate instead of fixed costs as a good number to use in a *break-even analysis*. In classic financial projections, the kind they still teach in financial analysis courses in business school, you'd use your fixed costs to calculate your break-even point. Burn rate is a newer and better—idea.

> **SUGGESTED READING**
> **BURN RATE**
>
> Michael Wolff was by no means the first or the only one to popularize the term *burn rate*, but his book, *Burn Rate: How I Survived the Gold Rush Years on the Internet*, cemented the term into the post-internet dotcom boom business vocabulary.

Estimate Spending Related to Sales

Some cost estimates go directly along with the sales forecast, because these are costs that you don't incur unless you make the sale. If you haven't already, you might want to read "Understanding Fixed and Variable Costs and Burn Rate" on page 148, with some important definitions. The sidebar on page 154 will help, too.

So I assume you already have your sales forecast. One of the first things you do with a spending budget is figure out how much it costs you to deliver what you're selling. As I explained in the previous section, this is cost of sales, sometimes called cost of goods sold (COGS) or direct costs, and traditionally means the costs of materials and production of the goods a business sells. In accounting, cost of sales belongs in the month in which the goods

A WORD ABOUT WORDS

DON'T CONFUSE COSTS AND EXPENSES

Stick with the way the accountants and financial analysts deal with cost of sales. You'll get into trouble if you don't. You want your definition to be the same as theirs to avoid any misunderstandings.

That means cost of sales, also called direct costs, direct cost of sales, or costs of goods sold, is the money it costs you to buy or produce the goods you sell or to deliver the services you sell. Please don't confuse this with sales and marketing expenses. Travel, meals, commissions, credit card merchant fees, and such are sales expenses, not cost of sales.

Confusing, yes, but we can't help it. That's the way these terms are used. You don't want to make your own meanings, even if they're logical, because if you need to produce more formal financial projections later on, you need your meanings to match what people expect.

or services are actually sold, regardless of when they were purchased or produced.

For a manufacturing company, this refers to materials, labor, and factory overhead. For a retail shop, it would be what the store pays to buy the goods that it sells to its customers. For a consulting company, the cost of sales would be the remuneration paid to the consultants plus costs of research, photocopying, and production of reports and presentations.

If you projected sales in units for your sales forecast, then it should be fairly easy (for most businesses) to figure out what each unit costs you. Then you can multiply that per-unit amount by the units to estimate the costs associated with exactly that month's worth of sales, which is the point. See Figure 4.16.

If you just project sales by the total amount, then try to estimate the related costs and—at least as much as you can—keep the costs

Sales Forecast				
	Jan	Dec	Year 1	Year 2
Unit Sales				
Direct Unit Costs	Jan	Dec	Year 1	Year 2
Systems	$1,700.00	$1,700.00	$1,700.00	$1,686.82
Service	$30.00	$30.00	$30.00	$30.00
Software	$120.00	$120.00	$120.00	$120.00
Training	$11.10	$11.10	$11.10	$11.10
Other	$90.00	$90.00	$90.00	$90.00
Direct Cost of Sales				
Systems	$144,500	$467,500	$3,833,500	$4,217,050
Service	$6,000	$10,290	$93,840	$180,000
Software	$18,000	$58,800	$477,600	$600,000
Training	$1,610	$2,220	$24,753	$44,400
Other	$14,400	$18,000	$190,980	$225,000
Subtotal Direct Cost of Sales	$184,510	$556,810	$4,620,673	$5,266,450

In this sample, there is a unit cost for each of the items the store sells, so you multiply the units from the sales forecast times the per-unit cost to automatically calculate the direct cost of sales.

Figure 4.16 **Sample Cost of Sales**

in these cases in the same month as the related sales. Don't go crazy with it, but try.

Do a Simple Expense Budget

OK, maybe my example in Figure 4.16 is a bit much, but planning is for everybody, all companies, not just the startups, so what the heck. It's a not-so-small company, but the math is still pretty obvious.

The point is that budgeting expenses is a matter of simple math, common sense, and reasonable guesses, without statistical analysis, mathematical techniques, or any past data. The mathematics is simple; sums of the rows and columns. You've seen it before.

And, as with the sales forecast, you really need to have some idea of these numbers. Either you get it from past data, or you get it from your experience in the industry, or from a partner or team member with experience, or you do some shoe-leather research. Try the reverse telephone tree technique. Look for standard industry data.

Also, remember that even in the worst case, with the roughest estimates, you have to go only one month without having any idea,

	Jan	Feb	Nov	Dec	Year 1
Payroll	$12,000	$12,000	$27,250	$27,250	$194,750
Advertising	$13,500	$13,500	$13,500	$13,500	$162,000
Leases	$500	$500	$500	$500	$6,000
Utilities	$1,000	$1,000	$1,000	$1,000	$12,000
Insurance	$300	$300	$300	$300	$3,600
Rent	$1,500	$1,500	$1,500	$1,500	$18,000
Payroll Tax	$1,680	$1,680	$3,815	$3,815	$27,265
Other	$0	$100	$200	$300	$1,000
Total	$30,480	$30,580	$48,065	$48,165	$424,615

Figure 4.17 **Sample Expense Budget**

because by the second month, with plan-as-you-go planning, you have the first month's results to help review and revise.

See Figure 4.17 for a simple expense budget.

Match the depth and detail of your budget to the control and accountability you have on your team. Make it so that the rows are useful for following up with later, looking at what was different from the plan and why.

Does your spending match your priorities? Remember the strategy pyramid, intended to help you keep your activities aligned with your strategy? This is where you begin to see it in action.

Aim for the right level of detail for following up. Too much detail makes it very hard to manage and track, and too much aggregation makes it hard to develop accountability. Do you know, in your business, who is responsible for each row in the budget? Does everybody else on the team know?

Personnel Plan					
	Jan	Nov	Dec	Year 1	Year 2
Partners	$12,000	$12,000	$12,000	$144,000	$175,000
Consultants	$0	$0	$0	$0	$50,000
Editorial/graphic	$0	$6,000	$6,000	$18,000	$22,000
VP Marketing	$0	$5,000	$5,000	$20,000	$50,000
Sales people	$0	$0	$0	$0	$30,000
Office Manager	$0	$2,500	$2,500	$7,500	$30,000
Secretarial	$0	$1,750	$1,750	$5,250	$20,000
Other	$0	$0	$0	$0	$0
Total People	3	7	7	7	14
Total Payroll	$12,000	$27,250	$27,250	$194,750	$377,000

Figure 4.18 **Sample Payroll Spreadsheet**

Before I go too much further, I'd like you to consider how important payroll is as part of you budget. Let's see where the payroll numbers in Figure 4.18 came from. I recommend you record these amounts in a separate table, whose totals flow into the expense budget table.

Estimate Your Payroll as Part of Expenses

Payroll is really the most important of your expenses, right? Unless you're working all alone, when things get fuzzier, the worst thing that can happen is missing payroll. So that's a number that should really be in your plan, among the simple basic numbers. I hope you agree.

Here too the math, the spreadsheet elements, are pretty simple. It doesn't take advanced analysis or specialized equations. If you have past data and history, it becomes very easy (which is not to say that projecting future pay increases is an easy part of business, but the math and estimation is relatively simple).

This is just one easy way to organize the data. Lots of people add sophistication to it, like dividing the payroll up into departments, or estimating how many people are in each functional area, then the average pay per person, then multiplying. For now, though, I want to keep things simple as we go.

Nobody Likes Budgets

It's funny how the words come together. Few people do projections, but lots of people do budgeting. They are not that much different. Lots of people hate to forecast. Lots of people hate budgets.

Even the word *budget* conjures up images of disapproving accountants and denied requests: "It's not in the budget" is one of the world's more familiar negatives. *No*, by any other name, would smell as sour.

> Your plan-as-you-go business plan should always include your spending budget.

But, despite their bad reputation, budgets are always useful tools and are almost essential to the proper running of a business. Budgets are used for planning and for tracking performance against plans. Your plan-as-you-go business plan should always include your spending budget, and that, by the way, when you rename it, is one of your building blocks for your projected income.

Some people think of budgets as normal, not scary. Some people think of forecasts as scary. They are basically the same thing.

Take it however it seems easier for you. It shouldn't be that hard to do.

The best and easiest way to create a useful expense budget is to take last year's expenses and run them forward.

Start with an empty spreadsheet, with the columns set up to show the months you're running for your plan, presumably 12 months. Then use the row labels on the leftmost column to assign categories. Start with something simple, like rent. Estimate your rent and get it into a standard format. Don't say you don't know or you have no idea. Take it a little bit at a time, and you'll have something you can work with.

The Budgeting Process

Here's a simple, step-by-step way to increase the importance of budgeting and implementation within your business.

1. *Preliminary budget meeting*. Start your budgeting process with a preliminary meeting that brings your main managers together. Discuss strategy and priorities, realistic amounts, and the planning process. Distribute a simple template and ask each manager to prepare a proposed budget for his area. Ask the managers to create a proposal that includes monthly numbers and descriptions of the programs and activities involved.

2. *Budget development*. Allow a period for managers to develop their budgets, working with the standard template. Enforce deadlines for preliminary proposals and revisions. Consolidate the proposed budgets into a single budget table that lists all of the suggested programs and activities. In most cases the total of all proposals will be two or three times the real amount your company can spend. Share that consolidated table with all managers. Share with them the difference between proposed budgets and actual spending limits, and ask them to think about it.

3. *Budget discussion*. Bring your managers back together to discuss the budget table. Ideally, you should set up a conference room with a projector and the consolidated proposed budget. Then you can go through the budget, item by item, and pare it down to a realistic amount. Your managers will be together in a group, so they will have to defend different proposals, and as they do they will build up their personal commitments and their ownership of budget items and programs. They will explain why one program is more valuable than another, they will argue about relative value, and they will increase the level of peer-group commitment.

When this process works well, you have a more accurate, more realistic, and more useful budget. You also have a high level of commitment from your managers, who are now motivated to implement the budget as well as possible.

Budgets and Milestones Work Together

Ideally, every line in a budget is assigned to somebody who is responsible for managing that budget. In most cases you'll have groups of budget lines assigned to specific people and a budgeting process that emphasizes commitment and responsibility. You'll also need to make sure that everybody involved knows that results will be followed up. The ideal plan relates the budgets to the milestones table, as in Figure 4.19. The milestones table takes all the important activities included in a business plan and assigns them to specific managers, with specific dates and budgets. It also tracks completion of the milestones and actual results compared with planned results.

The ideal plan relates the budgets to the milestones table.

The milestones are the heart and core of the business plan. Using the milestones table will assign responsibility and authority to the expense budget plans.

Milestones					
Milestone	**Start Date**	**End Date**	**Budget**	**Manager**	**Department**
Corporate Identity	28-Nov	14-Dec	$10,000	Tamzin J	Marketing
Seminar Implementation	29-Dec	7-Jan	$1,000	Irminsul R	Sales
Business Plan Review	30-Dec	8-Jan	$0	Reggie J	GM
Upgrade Mailer	30-Dec	14-Jan	$5,000	Irminsul R	Sales
New Corporate Brochure	30-Dec	14-Jan	$5,000	Tamzin J	Marketing
Delivery Vans	29-Dec	22-Jan	$12,500	Sepp D	Service
Direct Mail	30-Jan	14-Feb	$3,500	Isuldur R	Marketing
Advertising	30-Jan	14-Feb	$115,000	Reggie J	GM
X4 Prototype	29-Jan	22-Feb	$2,500	Geoffrey S	Product
Service Revamp	29-Jan	22-Feb	$2,500	Soren D	Product
6 Presentations	30-Jan	23-Feb	$0	Irminsul R	Sales
X4 Testing	27-Feb	4-Mar	$1,000	Geoffrey S	Product
3 Accounts	27-Feb	15-Mar	$0	SorenD	Sales
L30 Prototype	30-Mar	24-Mar	$2,500	Pamyla R	Product
Techo-Expo	30-Mar	10-Apr	$15,000	Todd B	Marketing
VP Sales & Marketing Hired	30-May	9-Jun	$1,000	Jemma K	Sales
Mailing System	29-Jun	23-Jul	$5,000	Sepp D	Service
Totals			**$181,500**		

Figure 4.19 **The Milestones Table**

Budgeting Is More About People than Numbers

While budget numbers are simple, budget management is not. To make a budget work, you need to add real management:

1. *Understand that it's about people.* Successful budgeting depends on people management more than anything else. Every budgeted item must be owned by somebody, meaning that the owner has responsibility for spending, authority to spend, and the belief that the spending limit is realistic. People who don't believe in a budget won't try to implement it. People who don't believe that it matters won't worry about a budget either.

2. *Budget ownership is critical.* To own a budget item is to have the authority to spend and the responsibility for that spending.

3. *Budgets need to be realistic.* Nobody really owns a budget item until she believes the budget amount is realistic. You can't really commit to a budget you don't believe in.

4. *It's also about following up.* Unless the people involved know that somebody will be tracking and following up, they won't

honor a budget. Publishing budget plan vs. actual results will make a world of difference. Rewards for budget success and penalties for budget failures can be as simple as meetings where peer group managers share results.

If You're Planning a New Business, Budget Your Startup Costs

There's a lot of potential confusion about startup costs. You tend to jump right into one of those accounting vocabulary problems that often trip people up, because they want to make things mean what they ought to mean, instead of what standard accounting and financial analysis make them mean.

> **NOT A STARTUP?**
>
> Go on. Jump to somewhere else in this book. This is one thing you don't have to worry about.

Startup costs include two kinds of spending. You might not care about the distinction, but standard accounting and finance do, and, more important, the government does. It affects taxes. So take a couple minutes to understand the distinction.

1. *Expenses.* These will be deductible against future profits, so they will eventually reduce taxes; at least they will if you ever make a profit. So keep track of expenses as expenses. These include spending on rent, payroll, travel, meals, consulting, most (but not all) legal expenses, and so on.

> **A WORD ABOUT WORDS**
>
> **WHICH IS IT?**
>
> Is it *start up* costs, *start-up* costs, or *startup* costs? I think spelling matters, so I apologize for the confusion there. I've decided to simplify my world and use *startup*. If that bothers you, I don't blame you. I like things in writing to go according to predictable rules. But sometimes the language just has to change. Sorry.

2. *Assets.* Money you spend on assets isn't deductible against taxable income, so the bookkeeping is different, like it or not. Assets are things like signs, furniture, fixtures, cars, trucks, buildings, land, and—harder to deal with—cash on hand and inventory on hand.

It seems like the toughest estimate to make is what you will need as cash on hand when you start the business. On the one hand, you have people telling you that you need working capital, and on the other, you have to raise it somehow or take it from your own savings and invest it in the business to make it cash on hand.

For expenses, timing is very important.

For expenses, timing is very important. Expenses like rent and payroll are startup expenses until your business is up and running; after that, they are just running expenses, which come out of your profits as deductible against income, so they reduce your taxable income. The only difference between rent paid before the company starts (which is a startup expense) and rent paid during the normal course of the business is timing. When it happens before day one, it's a startup expense. Afterward, it's a regular business expense.

If you are a startup, then your basic business numbers should include startup costs. Make two simple lists, one of expenses and the other one of assets. You'll need this information to set up initial business balances and to estimate startup expenses, such as legal fees, stationery design, and brochures. Don't underestimate costs.

Figure 4.20 is a typical startup table for a homebased office, service business—in this case, a resume writing service. The assumptions used in this illustration show how even simple, service-based businesses need some startup money.

You can see in the illustration how you have two simple lists, one for expenses and one for assets.

These are estimates. Where do they come from? Part of the planning for a startup is figuring these numbers out. Either you

Startup Plan	
Requirements	
Startup Expenses	
Legal	$1,000
Stationery, etc.	$3,000
Brochures	$5,000
Consultants	$5,000
Insurance	$350
Expensed Computer Equipment	$3,000
Other	$1,000
Total Startup Expenses	**$18,350**
Startup Assets	
Cash Required	$25,000
Other Current Assets	$7,000
Long-term Assets	$0
Total Assets	**$32,000**
Total Requirements	**$50,350**

Use a startup requirements worksheet like this to plan your initial financing.

Figure 4.20 **Startup Costs Table**

already have a pretty good idea, because you've worked in this area before, or you have somebody in the know, as partner, team member, advisor, or friend, who is helping you. You can also find some industry-specific startup information on the web and in bookstores. Sometimes a carefully selected sample business plan will help, but if you try that, be careful, because sample business plans are just about one case for one business at one specific location sometime in the past. They are not intended to stand for all businesses; you have to know your own case.

You might also make a separate list of the assets instead of just this summary. Other current assets, for example, are things that you need to buy but don't last long enough to be depreciated. That might be coffeemaking equipment, packaging equipment, some printing and layout materials, maybe chairs and tables as well.

**TIPS &
TRAPS**

ASSETS VS. EXPENSES

Many people can be confused by the accounting distinction between expenses and assets. For example, they would like to record research and development as assets instead of expenses, because those expenses create intellectual property. However, standard accounting and taxation law are both strict on the distinction:

- Expenses are deductible against income, so they reduce taxable income, but expenses cannot be depreciated, ever.

- Assets are not deductible against income, but assets whose value declines over time (usually long-term assets) can be depreciated.

Some people are also confused by the specific definition of startup expenses, startup assets, and startup financing. They would prefer to have a broader, more generic definition that includes, say, expenses incurred during the first year, or the first few months, of the plan. Unfortunately, this would also lead to double counting of expenses and nonstandard financial statements. All the expenses incurred during the first year have to appear in the profit and loss statement of the first year, and all expenses incurred before that have to appear as startup expenses.

This treatment is the only way to correctly deal with the tax implications and the proper assigning of expenses to the time periods in which they belong. Tax authorities and accounting standards are clear on this.

What a company spends to acquire assets is not deductible against income. For example, money spent on inventory is not deductible as an expense at the point when you buy it. Only when the inventory is sold, and therefore becomes cost of goods sold or cost of sales, does it reduce income.

Why You Do Not Want to Capitalize Expenses

Sometimes people want to treat expenses as assets. Ironically, that is usually a bad idea, for several reasons:

TIPS & TRAPS

ASSETS VS. EXPENSES, CONTINUED

■ Money spent buying assets is not tax deductible. Money spent on expenses is deductible.

■ Capitalizing expenses creates the danger of overstating assets.

■ If you capitalize the expense, it appears on your books as an asset. Having useless assets on the accounting books is not a good thing.

If you're looking at starting a company that has significant long-term assets, such as manufacturing equipment, vehicles, or land and buildings, you can also make a list of those.

You don't want to start a company without having a pretty good idea of what you have to spend to get it started.

Beware the Cash Traps

Profits aren't cash. Profits are an accounting concept; cash is what we spend. We pay the bills and payroll with cash. While the plan-as-you-go business plan doesn't necessarily include a full-blown financial forecast (at least not until needed) you should still be aware of cash balances and cash flow.

Profits are an accounting concept; cash is what we spend.

This should be a pretty simple concept, but it gets hard because we're trained to think about profits more than cash. It's the general way of the world. When they do the mythical business plan on a napkin, they think about what it costs to build something and how much more they can sell it for, which means profits.

However, you can be profitable without having any money in the bank. And what's worse is that it tends to happen a lot when

TRUE STORY

CASH FLOW PROBLEMS

This is a true story, although the names and places have been changed. Everything ended up OK, but there was a lot of unnecessary stress, all of which could have been easily prevented by just a minimum of business planning. This kind of problem happens all the time, and it's so easily preventable, it's a shame it happens at all. The lesson: Don't be a victim of unplanned growth.

The story takes place in a midsize university town on the West Coast, during the mid-'90s, as the internet boom took off and most everybody in business and education was getting connected. The main players are Leslie and Terry, co-owners of a consulting business offering computer and network services mostly to local businesses.

At the beginning of this story, Leslie and Terry had a small but comfortable office a few blocks off Main Street, near the university, and a comfortable business, averaging about $20,000 in sales per month with a few steady clients and not a lot of seasonal variations in sales. They had one employee who did the bookkeeping and general administration tasks, maintained office hours, and made appointments.

Then came the big, wonderful new job—a contract with a large and fast-growing company to install new internet facilities in offices on its corporate campus, ten miles up the freeway. This was a $200,000 contract that had to be delivered quickly and opened up an important new relationship with a potentially business-changing client. There was great celebration. Leslie and Terry and their spouses started with a fancy dinner in the best restaurant in the area.

Both partners readily got going on fulfilling the contract, delivering the network, connecting the systems, making good on their promises. To make sure the new relationship would result in a permanent increase in business, they took on five contractor consultants to deal with the needs of installation, training, and the general increase in business demands.

Within two months, it seemed clear to both partners that they'd made the leap. Systems were being installed, clients were happy, and they were on the road to doubling their business volume in a very short period of time. The contractors were doing good work, and four of the five

TRUE STORY

CASH FLOW PROBLEMS, CONTINUED

were happy to consider becoming permanent employees. Leslie and Terry decided they could celebrate more, so they both went to the local car dealer and leased new Mercedes sedans.

Then things started going bad. Like a television losing its connection, things got fuzzy, then blank. Though sales and profits were way up, jobs were done, and invoicing was under way, Leslie and Terry had no money. The contractors—good people who Leslie and Terry wanted to keep—needed to be paid, but there was no money. They rushed to their local bank, waving their increased sales and profits, but banks need time. The business suffered the classic problems of unplanned growth. Just as the accounting reports looked brightest, the coffers were empty. People were barely done celebrating, and suddenly they were looking at the disaster of unpaid bills and, much worse, unpaid people.

What happened? Unplanned cash-flow problems happened. The new, larger client had a slow process when it came to paying bills, so the jump in sales didn't mean an immediate jump in cash in the bank. Leslie and Terry were more concerned about delivering good service than delivering necessary paperwork, so their own invoicing process was slow. They were owed about $85,000, but they couldn't go straight to their new client to get the money—she said she'd already authorized payment and sent them to the company's finance department for answers. The people in the finance department were slow to respond and not particularly concerned about vendors getting paid quickly; their job was to pay slowly, but not so slowly as to get a bad credit rating.

Leslie and Terry had a bad case of "receivables starvation"—money that was owed to them was already showing in sales and profits, but not in the bank. It would have been predictable, and preventable, with a good plan.

In this case, fortunately, the two partners had enough house equity to get a quick loan and pay their contractors. The business was saved and grew, but not without a great deal of stress and strain, and even second mortgages.

TRUE STORY

CASH FLOW PROBLEMS, CONTINUED

The worst moment is worth remembering: One of the partners' spouses was particularly eloquent about the irony of taking on a new mortgage while driving that [profanity omitted] Mercedes.

The moral of the story: Always have a good cash-flow plan. Never get caught not knowing the impact of a sudden rush of new business. Get to the bank early, as soon as you know about new business, and start processing a credit line on receivables. And never lease a Mercedes until you're sure you won't have to take out a new mortgage a few weeks later.

Adapted from Entrepreneur.com column by Tim Berry, January 10, 2007.

you're growing, which turns good news into bad news and catches people unprepared.

Here are some traps you can watch for, to catch cash flow problems before they happen.

Every Dollar of Receivables Is a Dollar Less Cash

Although it's not intuitive, it's true that more receivables mean less cash. You can do the analysis pretty quickly. Assets have to be equal to capital minus liabilities, so if you have a dollar of receivables as an asset, that pretty much means you have one dollar less in cash. If your customers had paid you, it would be money, not accounts receivable.

This comes up all the time in business-to-business sales. In most of the world, when a business delivers goods or services to another business, instead of getting the money for the sale right away, there is an invoice and the business customer pays later. That's not always true, but it is the rule, not the exception. We call that *sales on credit*, by the way, and it has nothing to do with sales

TRUE STORY

RUN SILENT, RUN DEEP, RUN OUT OF MONEY

The most important problem is getting people who haven't been running companies to believe that cash flow and profits are different. That's so vitally important because, on the surface, it doesn't add up. It isn't believable.

I developed business planning software originally as templates for business-planning clients to deal with the following amazingly typical exchange:

> *Me*: So if you grow faster, then you'll need to get more financing.
>
> *Client*: No, that can't be true, because we're profitable. We make money with each sale, so the more we sell, the more we can fund ourselves.
>
> *Me*: Bingo! Please sit down here for a few minutes and deal with these numbers.

And so it would go. As soon as you're managing inventory or selling on credit—which means just about any sale you make to a business—then your cash flow is waiting in the wings, a silent killer, to foul you up.

I learned this first in business school and then forgot about it. I learned it later again, the hard way, when Palo Alto Software sales tripled in 1995 and that nearly killed the company. Why? How? Well, we experienced a huge sales increase by selling a software product through traditional channels of distribution, meaning stores, and that means selling to distributors who then resell to stores, and that means that it can take five months between selling the product and being paid for the product. In the meantime, you've got to make payroll and pay your vendors.

Yes, it's a good problem to have—we all want to increase our sales and profits—but it's a whole lot easier to deal with if you understand the plan for the cash implications well.

Often in presentations I use one of my favorite metaphors, the Willamette River as it runs through Eugene, Oregon, where I live. (See the photo.) The river slows down coming out of the Cascade Mountains and into Eugene, and it looks deep, slow, and peaceful, but it's much more dangerous there than when it's throwing up white water through the rapids. Why? Because it

RUN SILENT, RUN DEEP,
RUN OUT OF MONEY, CONTINUED

seems so calm and welcoming. People disrespect its currents, get caught in weeds, branches, or rocks, and . . . well that's a good metaphor for the way cash flow hits small businesses when things are good, when sales are growing.

What's particularly painful about the cash-flow problems that come with growth is that, precisely because there is growth, these problems can be prevented by planning.

You can see how the sales are growing, then determine what your cost of sales will be, and look at what you have to pay, to whom, and when. See how your checking account will balance will go down and down. Next, chart out when your customers will pay you. It will be obvious if you will run out of money before those profits actually reach your hands. You can then plan how to find the financing to float your boat before you actually hit the snag and sink.

We've had growth spurts since then that were far less painful because we understood the dangers of cash flow, planned for the cash implications of growth, and worked with our bank ahead of time to make sure the working capital was there.

paid for by credit card (which, ironically, is usually the same as cash less a couple of days and a couple of percentage points as fees).

We can use this in making financial projections: the more assets you have in receivables, the less in cash.

Example: A company running smoothly with an average of 45 days wait for its receivables has a steady cash flow with a minimum balance of just a little less than $500,000. The same company is more than half a million dollars in deficit when its collection

A WORD ABOUT WORDS

CRITICAL CASH VOCABULARY

These words put some people off because they sound like accounting and financial analysis. But they're good terms to know, especially if you're running a business.

Receivables is short for accounts receivable, which is money owed to you by customers who haven't paid yet.

Sales on credit isn't about credit cards, but rather business-to-business sales. It refers to when you deliver the goods and services to a business customer along with an invoice and don't get paid immediately. The amount you charge is considered accounts receivable until your business customer pays you.

Collection days refers to how long a business waits, on average, to get paid by its customers.

Inventory is stuff that you've purchased and you keep until you sell it to customers. That could be materials you're going to assemble into something or products you're going to sell to customers. Inventory is an asset. It doesn't become a cost until you sell it. Therefore it doesn't show up on the profit and loss statement until you sell it. But you probably have already paid for it.

Accounts payable is money you owe. When your business customers haven't paid you, what is accounts receivable to you is accounts payable to them.

period goes to 90 days instead of 45. That's a swing of more than a million dollars between the two assumptions. And that's in a company with less than $10 million annual sales and fewer than 50 employees.

And the trick is that the profit and loss statement doesn't care about receivables. You have as much profit when you sell $1,000 that your customers haven't paid yet as when you sell $1,000 that your customers paid instantly in cash. Obviously, the cash-flow implications are different in either case.

Every Dollar of Inventory Is a Dollar Less Cash

When your business has to buy stuff before it can sell it, that stuff is called inventory. It's one of your assets. And keeping a lot of inventory can do bad things to your cash flow, unless you don't pay for it.

This can be pretty simple math. If having nothing in inventory leaves you with $20,000 in cash, then having $19,000 in inventory leaves you with only $1,000 in cash. That is, if you've paid for the inventory. That's because your other assets, your liabilities, and your capital are all the same.

Sometimes, of course, you cannot pay for that inventory, which means you have more payables, and your cash balance is supported by those payables.

The difference in cash with different assumptions can be startling. You can look ahead to see this represented graphically in Figure 4.22.

Every Dollar of Payables Is a Dollar More of Cash

While receivables and inventory suck up money by dedicating assets to things that might have been cash but aren't, paying your own bills late is a standard way to protect your cash flow. The same basic math applies: if you leave your money in cash instead of using it to pay your bills, you have more cash.

> Every dollar in accounts payable is a dollar you have in cash that won't be there if you pay that bill.

It's called accounts payable, meaning money that you owe. Every dollar in accounts payable is a dollar you have in cash that won't be there if you pay that bill. The same problem you have when you sell to businesses is an advantage you have when you are a business. The seller's accounts receivable is the buyer's accounts payable.

Now I don't want to imply that you shouldn't pay your bills, or that paying on time it doesn't matter. Your business will have credit problems and a bad reputation if it doesn't pay bills on time, or if it is chronically late with the bills. Still, a lot of businesses use accounts payable to help finance themselves.

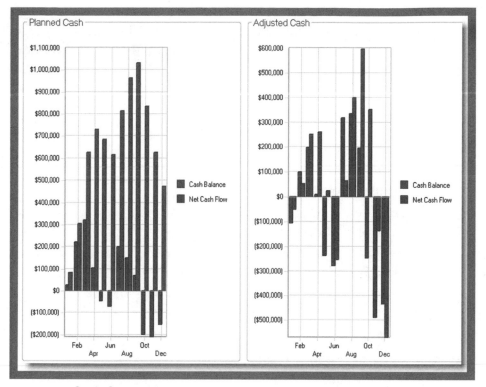

Figure 4.21 **Cash Scenarios**

Source: Business Plan Pro, AMT Sample Plan, Cash Pilot View. The cash pilot allows instant adjustment of critical cash variables, including sales on credit as a percent of sales, collection days, inventory on hand, and payment days. In this scenario, the business on the left experiences 45 collection days on average, and the one on the right experiences 90 days on average.

So What if You Wait a Bit Longer to Get Paid?

Does it matter if you wait longer to get paid by your customers? Only about a million dollars' worth. In the example shown in Figure 4.21, the company on the left gets paid by its customers in 45 days on average, and the one on the right in 90 days. Nothing else changes. Assumptions for sales, costs, expenses, and everything else are exactly the same. In the first case, the minimum cash balance is just less than half a million dollars, and in the second case, the one on the right, the cash balance is actually a deficit of more than half a million dollars.

Think of the implications. Both scenarios have the same sales of about $6 million per year, with the same profits of about 7 percent on sales. But the company on the left is doing just fine, and the company on the right is in real trouble, possibly going under.

Inventory: What a Difference Two Months Make

In the example in Figure 4.22, the company on the left keeps one month's worth of inventory, and the one on the right keeps three months. That's the only difference between both of these cash scenarios. The result of the three-month inventory assumption in this case is almost a million dollars of deficit by the end of the year.

Ten Rules for Managing Cash

Cash-flow problems can kill businesses that might otherwise survive. According to a U.S. Bank study, 82 percent of business failures are due to poor cash management. To prevent this from happening to your business, here are my ten cash-flow rules to remember.

1. *Profits aren't cash; they're accounting.* And accounting is a lot more creative than you think. You can't pay bills with profits. Actually, profits can lull you to sleep. If you pay your bills and your customers don't, it's suddenly business hell. You can make profits without making any money.
2. *Cash flow isn't intuitive.* Don't try to do it in your head. Making the sales doesn't necessarily mean you have the money. Incurring the expense doesn't necessarily mean you paid for it already. Inventory is usually bought and paid for and then stored until it becomes cost of sales.

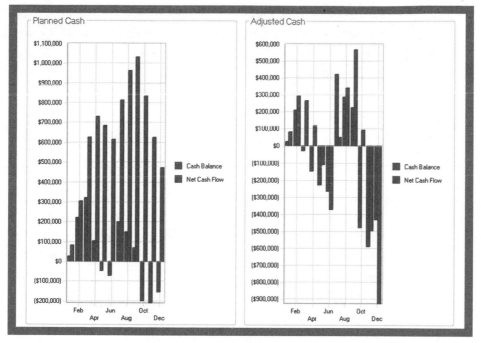

Figure 4.22 **Impact for More Inventory**

Source: Business Plan Pro, AMT Sample Plan, Cash Pilot View. The cash pilot allows instant adjustment of critical cash variables, including sales on credit as a percent of sales, collection days, inventory on hand, and payment days. In this scenario, the company on the left keeps a month of inventory on average, and the one on the right keeps three months of inventory on average.

3. *Growth sucks up cash.* It's paradoxical. The best of times can be hiding the worst of times. One of the toughest years my company had was when we doubled sales and almost went broke. We were building things two months in advance and getting the money from sales six months late. Add growth to that and it can be like a Trojan horse, hiding a problem inside a solution. Yes, of course you want to grow; we all want to grow our businesses. But be careful, because growth costs cash. It's a matter of working capital. The faster you grow, the more financing you need.

4. *Business-to-business sales suck up your cash.* The simple view is that sales mean money, but when you're a business selling to another business, it's rarely that simple. You deliver the goods or services along with an invoice, and they pay the invoice later. Usually that's months later. And businesses are good customers, so you can't just throw them into collections because then they'll never buy from you again. So you wait. When you sell something to a distributor that sells it to a retailer, you typically get the money four or five months later if you're lucky.

5. *Inventory sucks up cash.* You have to buy your product or build it before you can sell it. Even if you put the product on your shelves and wait to sell it, your suppliers expect to get paid. Here's a simple rule of thumb: Every dollar you have in inventory is a dollar you don't have in cash.

6. *Working capital is your best survival skill.* Technically, *working capital* is an accounting term for what's left over when you subtract current liabilities from current assets. Practically, it's money in the bank that you use to pay your running costs and expenses and buy inventory while waiting to get paid by your business customers.

7. *Receivables is a four-letter word.* (See rule 4.) The money your customers owe you is called accounts receivable. Here's a shortcut to cash planning: Every dollar in accounts receivable is a dollar less cash.

8. *Bankers hate surprises.* Plan ahead. You get no extra points for spontaneity when dealing with banks. If you see a growth spurt coming, a new product opportunity or a problem with customers paying, the sooner you get to the bank armed with charts and a realistic plan, the better off you'll be.

9. *Watch these three vital metrics. Collection days* is a measure of how long you wait to get paid. *Inventory turnover* is a measure of how long your inventory sits on your working capital

WHAT IF I DON'T KNOW

This headline caught you because you're planning something new. If you're planning something that's been around for a while, then you do know, or somebody knows, what you've been spending. That gives you past data to help with your planning.

So, for you newbies, first you should know that you're not the first. Everybody who plans something new has to go through that initial stage when you don't have past results as a base. So you estimate.

I get this complaint a lot: "I don't know what my costs are." Or, the interestingly naive alternative to that: "What will my costs be?" The answer is, you'd better know. Here again, if you're never going to get this and don't want to, but you believe in the business, then you either already have somebody who does this or you'd better find somebody and get him on the team. Teams, remember? Businesses don't have to be teams, but most of them are, and that's because people are different.

One way or another, if you're going to run your business, you're going to have to plan the ebb and flow of money. Deal with it. It's not that hard. Just break it down into pieces. Guess your rent first, or maybe your salaries. Utilities are fairly easy. Health insurance. Don't try to globally guess how much it will be altogether; break it into pieces. Your car. Gasoline and insurance. Maintenance.

And then follow up. Check your plan once a month, compare the plan with the actual results, and improve the plan. Nobody's supposed to know everything, and nobody knows the future, but you can keep making your projections better. The hardest is the first one, before you have any results. From there, things improve.

and clogs your cash flow. *Payment days* is how long you wait to pay your vendors. Always monitor these three vital signs of cash flow. Project them 12 months ahead and compare your plan with what actually happens.

10. *If you're the exception rather than the rule, hooray for you.* If all your customers pay you immediately when they buy from you, and you don't buy things before you sell them, then relax. But if you sell to businesses, keep in mind that they usually don't pay immediately.

Adapted with permission from an Entrepreneur.com column. All rights reserved.

It's Not Rocket Science

Please, recognize that you either have a pretty good idea of these numbers, or you'd better find out, or you aren't really running a business and you don't actually want to. Or there is somebody on your team who can do this. Or you have to find somebody on your team.

Dressing and Growing

A s your company grows, your planning grows. As you grow, if you add people to your team, then you want to bring them into the process, and make sure you're on the same page. You bring in skills.

The business gets more complex as it grows. Cash flow gets more sophisticated. You start to manage the money and administration differently.

Or you have a business plan event. You want or need to present a complete formal business plan, or the elevator speech, or the pitch presentation, or the summary memo.

That's what this section is about. Grow it and dress it as needed.

Item	Description
Financial Forecast	By the time you have the basic numbers in your evolving plan, it's not too hard to fill in some blanks and follow some standards to create a complete financial forecast. That's the projected income (profit and loss), balance sheet, cash flow, business ratios, the whole thing. It will make you look good and feel good to have a complete financial forecast.
Supporting Information	This is about the classic market analysis, industry analysis, and business descriptions: your management team, company history, and so on. Earlier I said this should be separate from your plan until you're going to use it. This is about how to do it when you need it.
Dress It as Needed	This is about the output. Having a plan, how to create an elevator speech, a pitch presentation, a summary memo, and of course the full formal business plan document.

From Basic Numbers to Financial Projections

There are some good reasons that you might need formal financial projections. The best reason is planning cash flow better. I wrote about the cash-flow traps in the previous chapter; being aware of them is better than not, but with standard financial projections, you can take your sales forecast, expense budgets, and starting position and with a few reasonable assumptions, you can project your cash. That, however, takes standard financial projections. The cash flow is like the link between your income and your balances. See Figure 5.1.

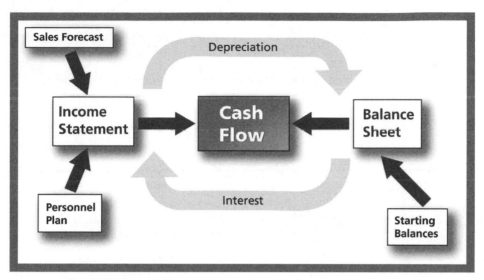

Figure 5.1 **Financial Projections**

If you've done the basic numbers, you're already more than half the way there. You've already estimated your future sales, cost of sales, and operating expenses. You're very close to a standard pro forma income statement. Just add projections for interest and taxes, and you have that done.

From there you want to project your balances. What will happen with capital, assets, and liabilities? If you can set your starting balances to match your beginning-of-the-plan estimated guesses,

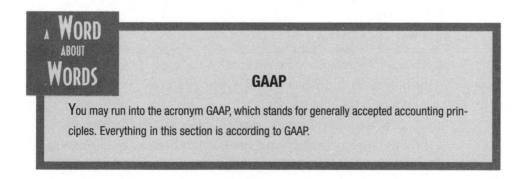

A WORD ABOUT WORDS

GAAP

You may run into the acronym GAAP, which stands for generally accepted accounting principles. Everything in this section is according to GAAP.

INCOME VS. BALANCE VS. CASH

An *income statement* (also called profit and loss) shows your business performance over a defined period of time (usually a month or a year). This is sales less costs less expenses, which equals profits.

A *balance sheet*, on the other hand, shows your financial position at some moment (usually at the end of the month or the end of the year). This is assets, liabilities, and capital. Assets must always be equal to capital (also called equity) and liabilities.

The *cash flow* reconciles the other two. Not all your money received nor all your spending shows up in the income statement, and not all of it shows up in the balance sheet. The cash flow links the two. And, much more important, it shows where the money comes from and where it goes.

then some rolling assumptions will take you right from there to cash.

In fact, my favorite way to make these estimates is to change and manage numbers in the cash flow and use those changes to automatically generate the balance sheet. I'll show you how to do this in detail in this section.

In the meantime, though, there are some standard conventions for the way these various statements link together. This is true in GAAP, in Excel, in Lotus 1-2-3 if you do it right, and automatically in Business Plan Pro.

■ *Your sales forecast should show sales and cost of sales.* The same numbers in the sales forecast are the ones you use in the profit and loss statement.

■ *As with sales, you should normally have a separate personnel table,* but the numbers showing in that table should be the same numbers that show up for personnel costs in your profit and loss table.

- *Your profit and loss table should show the same numbers as sales and personnel plan tables in the proper areas.* It should also show interest expenses as a logical reflection of interest rates and balances of debt.

- *Your cash flow has to reflect your profit and loss,* plus changes in balance sheet items and noncash expenses such as depreciation, which are on the profit and loss. The changes in the balance sheet are critical. For example, when you borrow money, it doesn't affect the profit or loss (except for interest expenses later on), but it makes a huge difference to your checking account balance.

- *The balance sheet has to reflect the profit and loss and the cash flow.*

- *Your business ratios should calculate automatically, based on the numbers in sales, profit and loss, personnel, cash flow, and balance sheet.*

Facts about Financial Projections

Normal people hate financial projections because of their off-putting formats and buzzwords. Really, it's just a matter of making good estimated guesses about what you're going to be selling, what it'll cost, and what your expenses will be.

Let's go over a few simple points that generate a lot of unnecessary errors in business plans. These are simple facts—accounting conventions, in some cases—that answer a lot of entrepreneurs' frequently asked questions. Don't let your business plan look bad because of easy-to-fix errors.

Before I start, take a breath. Don't glaze over when you see financial terms. They aren't that hard, and they are that important. Stick with me.

1. *Tax law allows businesses to establish so-called fiscal years instead of calendar years for tax purposes.* For example, your fiscal year might go from February through January, or October through September. Use FY (as in FY07) to specify the year in your plan. The fiscal year is always the calendar year in which a plan ends, not the year it starts.

2. *Understand sales on credit and accounts receivable.* When your business sells anything to another business, you usually have to deliver an invoice and wait to get paid. That's called sales on credit, which has nothing to do with credit cards, but plenty to do with B2B sales. When you make the sale and deliver the invoice, the invoice amount increases sales and accounts receivable. When that money gets paid, it decreases accounts receivable and increases cash.

3. *Separate costs from expenses.* Costs are normally the cost of sales, sometimes called cost of goods sold or direct costs. Costs are the money you spend on whatever you're selling, like what a bookstore pays to buy books. Expenses are regular running expenses like rent and payroll—expenses you'd have whether or not you had any sales.

4. *Don't call your investment venture capital unless it comes from one of the few hundred actual VC firms.* If you're getting venture capital, you'll know it. If not, just call it investment.

5. *Don't confuse assets with expenses.* New entrepreneurs think their companies look better if they have a lot of assets. One common example is wanting to take money spent on programmers and pretend that paying a programmer is buying an asset. Take my word for it: You don't really want that. It's better to expense those development expenses. That lowers your tax bill and makes your balance sheet look better, because you don't have fake assets.

6. *The two main accounting standards are either cash basis or accrual; accrual is better because it gives you more accurate cash*

projections. It seems counterintuitive, but cash basis isn't as good for predicting cash. The difference is timing. In accrual, the sale happens when you deliver the goods or perform the service. In cash basis, the sale happens when you get the money. In accrual, you owe the money when you receive the good or service, regardless of when you pay. In cash basis, you don't show what you owe until you pay it. I strongly recommend accrual because it's much more realistic. Real businesses don't pay upfront; they pay later.

7. *Pro forma is just a dressed-up way to say projected or forecast.* It's one of those potentially daunting buzzwords that really isn't that complicated. The pro forma income statement, for example, is the same as the projected profit and loss or the profit and loss forecast.

> The pro forma income statement is the same as the projected profit and loss or the profit and loss forecast.

Adapted from Entrepreneur.com column, May 2007.

Projections: How Many Months? How Many Years?

For any normal planning purposes, for any normal company, you should have at least 12 months detailed month by month for business plan forecasts. That would be for sales forecast, cost of sales, your burn rate, and eventually the complete financial forecast, if you're going to do it. Then have another two years beyond that, for three years total, as annual projections.

That doesn't mean you don't think in longer terms. Think about what you want for your business for 5, 10, or 20 years. I'm all in favor of that. But I don't think you should plan in the detail of financial forecasts for very long time periods. The larger numbers—sales, for example—involve so much uncertainty that you don't get your time's worth back by trying to project more detail. At least not in normal cases. If you're farming lumber from tree farms, maybe.

Be forewarned. You'll run into experts who will say you need more than 24 months by month, or more than five years in detail. They will be very sure of themselves. Sometimes what they mean when they say that is that they know more than you do, so they want you to suffer more. Or they want you to pay them to do the financials instead. Or they don't like you or your business plan and they're embarrassed to tell you that. So instead, they say you need to forecast in more detail. If they are investors, what they mean is that they don't want to invest and they don't want to tell you why. If they are loan managers, they don't want to make the loan. And they don't want to tell you the real reason.

My advice to you, when that comes up, is that unless you are a special case (if you are, you know you are), look for another expert.

The Three Main Statements

I've taken you this far with just the basic business numbers. To be fair, that's far enough. It certainly gives you some numbers to get a hold on and to manage, review, correct, and revise.

It's likely that at some point you'll want to go further, into the straight financial projections that are part of a complete formal business plan.

The good news is that with what we did with the basic numbers, you're already a long way there.

The bad news is that here again the details and specific meanings of financial terms matter. You can't just guess. I warned you earlier about the importance of timing with sales, costs, and expenses. This is very true with standard financials. Also, it starts to matter what goes where. It can be confusing and annoying. For example, interest expense goes into the income statement but principal repayment goes into the cash flow, which then affects the balance, but never appears anywhere in income. That means a standard debt payment that includes both interest and principal repayment has to be divided up into both parts. Interest is an expense on the profit and loss. Debt payment reduces debt on the balance sheet.

Elsewhere in this book I discuss the huge difference between planning and accounting. With the three main financial statements, specifically, financial analysts use the term *pro forma* to describe projected statements and predictions. An income statement, for example, is about past results. A pro forma income statement is a projected income statement.

The Income Statement

The income statement is also called profit and loss. People often refer to the bottom line as profits, the bottom line of the income statement. It has a very standard form. It shows sales first, then cost of sales (or cost of goods sold, or direct costs, which is essentially the same thing). Then it subtracts costs from sales to calculate gross margin (which is defined as sales less cost of sales). Then it shows operating expenses, usually (but not always) subtracting operating expenses from gross margin to show EBIT (earnings before interest and taxes). Then it subtracts interest and taxes to show profit.

Sales – Cost of Sales = Gross Margin

Gross margin – Expenses = Profits

Notice that the income statement involves only four of the seven fundamental financial terms (page 204). While an income statement will have some influence on assets, liabilities, and capital, it includes only sales, costs, expenses, and profit.

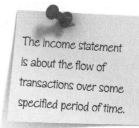

The income statement is about the flow of transactions over some specified period of time.

The income statement is about the flow of transactions over some specified period of time, like a month, a quarter, a year, or several years.

PROFIT, INCOME, AND SO ON

Some say income statement, some say profit & loss, or profit or loss. That's the same thing. Accountants and financial analysts use those titles interchangeably. I use income and income statement, but you can read profit & loss if you like.

If you've done the basic numbers I recommended in the previous chapter—sales and cost of sales in the sales forecast and expenses (including payroll)—then you've got the bulk of the income statement done. Take the sales and cost of sales from that table, and the expenses from that table, and if you have interest expenses, and taxes, add them in. And that's about what it takes.

The Balance Sheet

The most important thing about a balance sheet is that it includes a lot of spending and money management that isn't included in the income statement. It's most of the reason that profits are not cash, and that cash flow isn't intuitive. It's all very much related to the cash traps.

The balance sheet shows a business's financial position, which includes assets, liabilities, and capital, on a specified date. It will always show assets on the left side or on the top, with liabilities and capital on the right side or the bottom.

Balance sheets must always obey the following formula:

$$\text{Assets} = \text{Liabilities} + \text{Capital}$$

Unless that simple equation is true, the balance sheet doesn't balance and the numbers are not right. You can use that to help make estimated guesses and pull things together for projected cash flow.

The Cash Flow Statement

The cash flow statement is the most important and the least intuitive of the three. In mathematical and financial detail it reconciles the income statement with the balance sheet, but that detail is hard to see and follow. What is most important is tracking the money. By cash I mean liquidity, as in the balance in checking and related savings accounts, not strictly bills and coins. And tracking that cash is the most important thing a business plan does. The underlying truth is this:

Ending Cash = Starting Cash + Money Received – Money Spent

What's particularly important in planning is that neither the income statement alone nor the balance sheet alone is sufficient to plan and manage cash. I discuss the cash flow in much greater detail in the section that starts on page 194.

Standard Tables and Charts

So those three main tables are just about essential for a complete business plan: you have to project income, balance, and cash flow. Cash flow is the single most important numerical analysis in a plan and should never be missing. Most plans will also have a sales forecast and profit and loss statements. I believe they should also have separate personnel listings, a projected balance sheet, projected business ratios, and market analysis. There are others that are common, but not necessarily required (depending on the situation and exact context of the plan). Those might include the following:

■ *Startup costs and startup funding.* We've already talked about startup costs, but most business plans for startups also need to show where the money to pay for startup costs is coming from. That's a combination of investment and borrowed money. Your balances have to balance, and they don't balance without startup funding. Sometimes the startup funding will produce a useful business chart, a bar chart showing investment vs. borrowed money.

- *Past performance.* When a plan is doing a complete financial forecast for an existing company, past performance is required to set the starting balances for the future. The last balance of the past is the first balance of the future. In practice, people often have to project a few months forward to estimate what the final balance will be on the day the new plan starts. For example, if you're doing a plan for next year starting in January, and it's only October, then you have to guess what will happen to balances between October and December.

- *Break-even analysis.* A break-even analysis is a standard routine that compares sales with fixed and variable costs to determine how much sales it will take to cover costs. It can be an annoying analysis sometimes, because it requires averaging variable costs and unit prices over an entire business, but it can still be useful as a first look at the risks related to fixed and variable costs.

- *Market analysis.* The market analysis is usually an important core component of the market information, supporting information that is required when you're working on a plan for outsiders. Investors, bankers, professors of business, consultants, and others like to see proof of market. The market analysis table shows what data you have, usually a market growth projection, in general by segment. It's really a good idea to break the market into useful subsets, called segments. Market analysis can produce some good-looking charts, too, like pie charts breaking the market into segments and bar charts showing market growth as projected into the future.

- *Ratios analysis.* When you're projecting your income and balances, you can then use math and formulas to project standard business ratios. There are a couple dozen standard ratios that accountants and analysts often like to see. These are things like return on investment, profits to sales, inventory turnover, collection days, and so on.

■ *Use of funds.* For plans intended to go to either investors or lenders, use of funds is a list showing how the money coming in will be spent. Use this to convince investors that you wll put their money to good use.

You should also use business charts, like bar charts and pie charts, to illustrate your projected numbers as much as possible. Graphics illustrate numbers very well. They are easier than numbers alone to see and understand.

Focusing on the Income Statement

The income statement is probably the most standard of all financial statements. It comes with standard math, too.

Sales – Cost of Sales = Gross Margin

Gross Margin – Operating Expenses = EBIT

EBIT is also called gross profit in some circles, but that same term is sometimes applied to the gross margin, so I like EBIT better.

EBIT – Interest – Taxes = Net Profit

The numbers are usually presented in that order. For financial statements, the presentation can become very complex, as various items get broken down into rows and rows of detail, but for planning purposes, you want to keep it simple if you can.

Figure 5.2 shows a simple income statement. This example doesn't divide operat-

---

GROSS MARGIN

I didn't talk much about gross margins when we discussed the sales forecast and the cost of sales, but the gross margin is a useful basis for comparison. Generally, industries have some kind of standard gross margin. Retail sporting goods do about 34 percent on average, and grocery stores about 20 percent. Your own results will always be different from the standard, so just understand why you're different, and don't worry about it too much.

	Jan	Feb	Mar
Sales	$70,000	$71,300	$72,600
Direct Cost of Sales	$15,000	$15,000	$15,000
Other	$1,000	$1,000	$1,000
Total Cost of Sales	$16,000	$16,000	$16,000
Gross Margin	$54,000	$55,300	$56,600
Gross Margin %	77.14%	77.56%	77.96%
Expenses			
Payroll	$29,750	$29,750	$29,750
Advertising	$14,000	$14,000	$14,000
Depreciation	$0	$0	$0
Leases	$500	$500	$500
Utilities	$1,100	$1,100	$1,100
Insurance	$300	$300	$300
Rent	$1,600	$1,600	$1,600
Payroll Tax	$4,500	$4,500	$4,500
Other	$0	$0	$0
Total Operating Expenses	$51,750	$51,750	$51,750
Interest Expenses	$617	$617	$617
Taxes Incurred	$408	$733	$1,058
Net Profit	$1,225	$2,200	$3,175

This is a partial graphic, showing only 3 months of a 12-month table.

Figure 5.2 **Standard Income Statement**

ing expenses into categories. The format and math start with sales at the top.

I hope you notice that you've already gathered most of this data as part of your flesh and bones of the plan. You've already done the sales forecast, cost of sales, payroll, and expenses. If you've followed the standard financial definitions, as I hope you did (otherwise I'll have to say I told you so), then creating the income statement is a matter of pulling the information together into a single table. Then add estimates of interest expense, and taxes.

Keep your assumptions simple. Remember our principle about planning and accounting. Don't try to calculate interest based on a complex series of debt instruments; just average your interest over the projected debt. Don't try to do graduated tax rates; just use an average tax percentage for a profitable company.

Keep Your Balance Sheet Simple

A business's balance sheet shows the financial picture at some specific time, like at the end of the last day of the month or the end of the last day of the year. The financial picture is a matter of assets, liabilities, and cap-

> ### THE LAW OF BALANCE
>
> Assets are always equal to the sum of capital and liabilities. Your books have to show that.

ital. Through the magic of double-entry bookkeeping, your financial transactions are recorded in a way that ensures the balance sheet will indeed balance if the entries are correct.

So let's make sure first that you know what's what. Some definitions are in order. These are three terms you should know in order to create a balance sheet:

- *Assets*. Cash, accounts receivable, inventory, land, buildings, vehicles, furniture, and other things the company owns are assets. Assets can usually be sold to somebody else. One definition is "anything with monetary value that a business owns."
- *Liabilities*. Debts, notes payable, accounts payable, amounts of money owed to be paid back.
- *Capital* (also called equity). Ownership, stock, investment, retained earnings. Actually there's an iron-clad and never-broken rule of accounting: Assets = Liabilities + Capital. That means you can subtract liabilities from assets to calculate capital.

This is planning, not accounting. That's one of the primary principles of the plan-as-you-go business plan. To make a powerful and useful cash-flow projection, you need to summarize and aggregate the rows of the balance sheet. Resist the temptation to break it down into detail the way you would with a tax report after the fact. This is a tool to help you forecast your cash. See Figure 5.3.

Pro Forma Balance Sheet				
		Jan	Feb	Mar
Assets	**Starting Balances**			
Current Assets				
Cash	$55	$1	$197	$376
Accounts Receivable	$395	$426	$511	$634
Inventory	$805	$621	$378	$332
Other Current Assets	$25	$25	$25	$25
Total Current Assets	$1,280	$1,073	$1,111	$1,367
Long-term Assets				
Long-term Assets	$350	$375	$375	$390
Accumulated Depreciation	$50	$51	$52	$53
Total Long-term Assets	$300	$324	$323	$337
Total Assets	$1,580	$1,397	$1,434	$1,704
Liabilities and Capital		Jan	Feb	Mar
Current Liabilities				
Accounts Payable	$224	$34	$49	$290
Current Borrowing	$90	$90	$90	$0
Other Current Liabilities	$15	$22	$22	$22
Subtotal Current Liabilities	$329	$146	$161	$312
Long-term Liabilities	$285	$282	$279	$376
Total Liabilities	$614	$428	$440	$688
Paid-in Capital	$500	$500	$525	$525
Retained Earnings	$418	$467	$467	$467
Earnings	$49	$1	$2	$25
Total Capital	$967	$968	$994	$1,017
Total Liabilities and Capital	$1,581	$1,396	$1,434	$1,705
Net Worth	$966	$969	$994	$1,016

Figure 5.3 **Standard Balance Sheet**

Keep your balance sheet simple because you need to link it to your cash-flow assumptions.

Planning the Cash Flow

I worry most about cash flow because it's so insidious. Like the old saying about rivers, still waters run deep. Cash is frequently hardest to manage when businesses are growing. It is the least intuitive of the financial projections, but the most important. I hope you've read through the cash-flow traps portion of Chapter 4. I was trying to scare you. It's good for you.

We got through the basic business numbers with that discussion of cash traps instead of the full detail of the cash flow. That might be enough for the early plan, but eventually you're going to want to build a real cash plan, using real numbers and real financial math.

Experts can be annoying. There are several ways to do a cash-flow plan. Sometimes it seems like as soon as you use one method, somebody who is supposed to know tells you you've done it wrong. Often that means she doesn't know enough to realize that there is more than one way to do it.

Let's start simple here, with a basic direct cash-flow plan. See Figure 5.4.

Even at this basic level, you can see the potential complications and the need for linking up the numbers using a computer. Your estimated receipts from accounts receivable must have a logical relationship to sales and the balance of accounts receivable. Likewise, your payments of accounts payable have to relate to the balances of payables and the costs and expenses that cre-

Cash Flow				
Money Received	Start	Month 1	Month 2	Month 3
Cash Sales	$0	$0	$0	$0
Payments Received	$0	$0	$75	$188
New Loans	$200	$0	$0	$0
New Investment	$300	$0	$0	$0
Total Received	$500	$0	$75	$188
Money Spent				
Cash Spending	$0	$0	$25	$50
Bill Payment	$0	$0	$300	$250
Repay Loans	$0	$0	$0	$0
Purchase Assets	$0	$0	$0	$0
Total Spent	$0	$0	$325	$300
Cash Flow	$500	$0	($250)	($113)
Cash Balance	$500	$500	$250	$138

Figure 5.4 **Simple Cash-Flow Plan**

There's nothing particularly fancy about this plan, or the table, or the math. You just need to keep track of money coming in and money going out. This means paying bills as they come due (i.e., paying accounts payable), and paying off loans.

ated the payables. Vital as this is to business survival, it is not nearly as intuitive as the sales forecast, personnel plan, or income statement. The mathematics and the financial projections are more complex.

Cash from Receivables

The row labeled, "Payments Received" contains estimates of the dollar amounts received from customers as payments of accounts receivable. This is critical to your cash flow. Estimating money from receivables is vital. You should estimate receivables using assumptions nimble enough to offer a useful estimate, but simple enough to manage. For example, in the sample case illustrated in Figure 5.5, I used estimated collection days to calculate amounts received as a manner of estimating the time that passed between making the sale and receiving the payment.

The collection-days estimator sets the amounts received. (Amounts shown in thousands. Numbers may be affected by rounding.)

The calculation in the example in Figure 5.5 is relatively simple. You can see how each month starts with beginning balance, adds new sales on credit, subtracts money received, and then calculates the ending balance. Notice that the amounts received in March are

Receivables Detail	Mar	Apr	May
Estimated Collection Period in Days	60	60	60
Sales on Credit %	85.00%	85.00%	85.00%
Receivables			
Beginning Receivables Balance	$511	$636	$942
Plus Sales on Credit	$353	$596	$547
Less Cash from Receivables	$228	$291	$353
Ending Receivables Balance	$636	$942	$1,136

Figure 5.5 **Sample Case: Receivables Detail**

the same as the sales on credit for January, because the collection-days estimator is set to 60 days.

To emphasize the importance of collection days as an estimator, look at Figure 5.6, which is set to 90 days instead of 60 days. In this case, sales on credit from March are received a month later, in April.

Receivables Detail			
	Mar	Apr	May
Estimated Collection Period in Days	90	90	90
Sales on Credit %	85.00%	85.00%	85.00%
Receivables			
Beginning Receivables Balance	$651	$865	$1,233
Plus Sales on Credit	$353	$596	$547
Less Cash from Receivables	$139	$228	$291
Ending Receivables Balance	$865	$1,233	$1,489

Figure 5.6 **Importance of Collection Days as an Estimator**

In this scenario, when collection days are stretched, less cash comes in from receivables. The difference affects cash flow. (Amounts shown in thousands. Numbers may be affected by rounding.)

This simple change turns acceptable cash flow into cash problems (see the section "So What if You Wait a Bit Longer to Get Paid?" on page 173).

Estimating Expenditures

The first two rows in the cash flow table in Figure 5.7, "Cash Spending" and "Bill Payment" record spending from normal operations. They can be linked to spending in the income statement through assumptions for bill payments and inventory management. The other ways to spend money are not included in the income statement.

Cash Flow			
Expenditures	Jan	Feb	Mar
Expenditures from Operations			
Cash Spending	$47	$47	$47
Bill Payment	$225	$36	$59
Subtotal Spent on Operations	$272	$83	$106
Additional Cash Spent			
Non Operating (Other) Expense	$0	$0	$0
Sales Tax, VAT, HST/GST Paid Out	$0	$0	$0
Principal Repayment of Current Borrowing	$0	$0	$90
Other Liabilities Principal Repayment	$0	$0	$0
Long-term Liabilities Principal Repayment	$3	$3	$3
Purchase Other Current Assets	$0	$0	$0
Purchase Long-term Assets	$25	$0	$15
Dividends	$0	$0	$0
Subtotal Cash Spent	$300	$86	$213

Figure 5.7 **Sample Case: Cash Spent**

The cash plan has to deal with the real flow of money spent. (Amounts shown in thousands. Numbers may be affected by rounding.)

1. The first row is "Cash Spending," which is money spent immediately to pay expenses that are not invoiced (due at a later date). The most obvious example is the spending for wages and salaries and other compensation-related payments you make every month to your employees and the government. These obligations don't go into accounts payable. Instead, you pay them every month. In most companies you can assume that wages and related personnel expenditures are paid the same month they're incurred.

2. The second obvious use of cash is bill payment. This accounts payable balance is money you owe. Every month, you pay off most of this, depending on how quickly you pay. I recommend estimating payments based on some simple calculations that depend on estimated average payment days, as shown in Figure 5.8.

Payment Detail			
	Jan	Feb	Mar
Payment Delay in Days	30	30	30
Payables			
Beginning Payables Balance	$224	$34	$49
Plus New Payment Obligations	$82	$97	$346
Less Cash Spending	$47	$47	$47
Less Bill Payments	$225	$36	$59
Ending Payables Balance	$34	$49	$290

Figure 5.8 **Payment Detail**

Payment delays affect cash flow. The calculations in Figure 5.8 are based on the assumption that payments are made 30 days after bills are received. (Amounts shown in thousands. Numbers may be affected by rounding.)

In the example here, the calculations start with the ending balance of accounts payable from the previous month, then add new obligations, then subtract obligations paid directly in cash, as well as this month's bill payments, to calculate this month's ending balance. This month's bill payments depend on the assumption of waiting 30 days, on average, before paying bills.

Additional Expenditures

Here's a breakdown of the items listed under "Additional Cash Spent" in Figure 5.7.

1. The "Non Operating (Other) Expense" row includes expenses outside of normal operations. This row is there to accommodate companies that have "Other Expenses" sections in their normal accounting statements. You know who you are, and if this isn't you, it doesn't affect you.

2. There is a row for spending related to sales tax and value-added tax (VAT), which is money a company holds because it collects it for the government, but which must, in turn, be

repaid. Normal cash flow tracks these tax-related amounts as they enter and leave the company.

3. The next three rows, "Principal Repayment of Current Borrowing," "Other Liabilities Principal Repayment," and "Long-Term Liabilities Principal Repayment," are for principal repayments of debt. When you pay off your loans, you lose cash. In the example, there is a regular payoff of $3,000 long-term debt, and a single payoff of $90,000 of the current (short-term) debt.

4. In the third row from the bottom, you record the purchase of new other current assets. You'll have to know how much you purchase in new assets in order to estimate your balance sheet. While in real life these might also be recorded as accounts payable and paid a few weeks later, we make them explicit here as if they were paid immediately in cash. That makes for better cash planning.

5. Logically, the next row is for purchases of new long-term assets. These also reduce cash.

6. The last row in spending tracks dividends. Dividends are the distribution of profits to owners and investors. They reduce cash but don't appear anywhere else.

Cash Received

Figure 5.9 lists possible cash sources for our sample company. Most of these have balance sheet impact, and several come from the income statement. For now, we'll focus just on the cash flow.

In this section of the cash-flow table, we list money received, such as cash sales and monies received from accounts receivable. (Amounts shown in thousands. Numbers may be affected by rounding.)

1. The first row, "Cash Sales," is a simple estimate. It should link with your sales forecast and income statement to avoid

Cash Flow			
Cash Received	Jan	Feb	Mar
Cash from Operations			
Cash Sales	$40	$51	$62
Cash from Receivables	$198	$205	$230
Subtotal Cash from Operations	$238	$256	$292
Additional Cash Received			
Non Operating (Other) Income	$0	$0	$0
Sales Tax, VAT, HST/GST Received	$0	$0	$0
New Current Borrowing	$0	$0	$0
New Other Liabilities	$0	$0	$0
New Long-term Liabilities	$0	$0	$100
Sales of Other Current Assets	$0	$0	$0
Sales of Long-term Assets	$0	$0	$0
New Investment Received	$0	$25	$0
Subtotal Cash Received	$238	$281	$392

Figure 5.9 **Sample Case: Cash Received**

inconsistencies. Normally, credit card sales are grouped into cash sales because the business gets the money in a day or two. "Cash" in this case means cash, check, and credit card, everything except the real sales on credit, in which the product or service changes hands in advance of the payment.

Additional Cash Received

In Figure 5.9, the first two rows in the "Cash from Operations" section are directly related to standard operations. Cash sales plus cash from receivables (sales on credit) equals total cash from operations (also known as total sales). The following rows are less direct and less readily available from simple assumptions. So I set these aside as "Additional Cash Received."

1. The third row, "Non-Operating (Other) Income," gives you a place to show money received from special operations, such as interest income in a company whose main business isn't making interest. A lot of businesses won't include this row.

2. The next row shows money received from charging customers sales-related and value-added (VAT) taxes that really belong to the government and must be paid later. These taxes aren't normally part of a sales forecast, so they don't affect the income statement, but they do affect cash flow.

3. The next three rows are where you estimate amounts of money coming into the company as new borrowed money. The difference between each of the three is a matter of type of borrowing and terms.

   • The row named "New Current Borrowing" (also called short-term debt) is for money you get by borrowing through normal lending institutions, such as standard loans, with interest payments.

   • The row named "New Other Liabilities" is for items like accrued taxes and accrued salaries and wages, money owed that will have to be paid but isn't formally borrowed. Normally there are no interest expenses associated with the money recorded in this row.

   • The row named "New Long-Term Liabilities" is for new money borrowed on longer terms. This type of borrowing usually requires interest payments.

4. The sixth and seventh additional cash rows are "Sales of Other Current Assets" and "Sales of Long-Term Assets." Selling short-term or long-term assets is another possible way to generate cash.

5. The last row, "New Investment Received," is for new money coming into the company as investment.

The result of this section is the sum of cash received. These are amounts received from normal operations (cash sales and cash from receivables) and additional amounts from assumptions outside the normal operations.

Planning for Inventory

Inventory (sometimes called stock), is the accounting term for goods or materials a company holds temporarily and then sells to its customers. For example, inventory in a bookstore is the value of the books the store owns and intends to sell to its customers. Inventory in a car dealership is unsold cars. Inventory in a steel manufacturing plant includes iron ore and coal to be made into steel.

Inventory goes into the financials as an asset when it's purchased. It is recorded as cost of goods sold when it's sold. The cost of inventory shows up in the cash flow when it's paid for, regardless of when it's sold, usually as cash spending or bill payments.

Not all companies manage inventory. Product-related companies normally do have inventory, and service-related companies normally don't. There are many exceptions, though, so if you have doubt, ask your accountant or somebody connected to your company who knows.

Use simple assumptions to estimate inventory flow and inventory purchases. (See Figure 5.10. Amounts shown in thousands. Numbers may be affected by rounding.)

Inventory gets into your cash flow when you pay for it. Estimate your inventory needs as months of inventory on hand, then estimate inventory flow as a matter of estimating sales and inventory

Inventory Detail	Jan	Feb	Mar
Months of Inventory On-hand	1.1	1.1	1.1
Minimum Inventory Purchase	$1,000		
Inventory Balance			
Beginning Inventory Balance	$805	$621	$378
Less Inventory Used as COGS	$185	$243	$302
Plus Inventory Purchase	$0	$0	$256
Ending Inventory Balance	$621	$378	$332

Figure 5.10 **Estimating Inventory**

A WORD ABOUT WORDS

SEVEN SIMPLE WORDS YOU SHOULD KNOW

You don't have to be an accountant or an MBA to do a business plan, but you will be better off with a basic understanding of some essential financial terms. Otherwise, you're doomed to either having somebody else develop and explain your numbers or having your numbers be incorrect. This is a good point to note the advantage of teams in business: if you have somebody on your team who knows fundamental financial estimating, then you don't have to do it yourself.

It isn't that hard, and it's worth knowing. If you are going to plan your business, you will want to plan your numbers. So there are some terms to learn. I'm not going to get into formal business or legal definitions, and I will use examples.

1. *Assets*. Cash, accounts receivable, inventory, land, buildings, vehicles, furniture, and other things the company owns are assets. Assets can usually be sold to somebody else. One definition is "anything with monetary value that a business owns."

2. *Liabilities*. Debts, notes payable, accounts payable, amounts of money owed to be paid back.

3. *Capital (also called equity)*. Ownership, stock, investment, retained earnings. Actually there's an iron-clad and never-broken rule of accounting: Assets = Liabilities + Capital. That means you can subtract liabilities from assets to calculate capital.

4. *Sales*. Exchanging goods or services for money. Most people understand sales already. Technically, the sale happens when the goods or services are delivered, whether or not there is immediate payment.

5. *Cost of sales (also called cost of goods sold, direct costs, and unit costs)*. The raw materials and assembly costs, the cost of finished goods that are then resold, the direct cost of delivering the service. This is what the bookstore paid for the book you buy, it's the gasoline and maintenance costs of a taxi ride, it's the cost of printing, binding, and royalties when a publisher sells a book to a store for resale.

purchases. Payments depend on the rest of your payments policy, because inventory purchase amounts enter the system when an invoice is received, but they are paid when the related invoices are paid.

In Figure 5.10, the beginning inventory balance supplies the amounts required until the third month, when additional inventory is purchased. That purchase goes into accounts payable and is paid as part of the normal flow of bill payments. Inventory purchase makes up the bulk of the $346,000 new obligations in March shown in Figure 5.8.

A More Realistic Example

The cash plan can get complicated quickly when you deal with a more realistic business example. In the following illustrations, we're going to look at the cash planning for the company whose cash balances were described in the cash flow sections in Chapter 4. This was the company whose cash flow varied widely, depending on cash assumptions.

Beginning Assumptions

With Figures 5.11 and 5.12 we set the starting points, which are the projected income and the starting balance. I've provided a simple

Income Statement	Jan	Feb	Mar	Apr
Sales				
Cash Sales	$40	$51	$62	$106
Sales on Credit	$228	$291	$354	$596
Total Sales	**$268**	**$342**	**$416**	**$702**
Direct Cost of Sales	$183	$242	$301	$392
Personnel in Cost of Sales	$10	$10	$10	$10
Other Cost of Sales	$1	$1	$1	$1
Total Cost of Sales	**$194**	**$253**	**$312**	**$402**
Gross Margin	**$74**	**$89**	**$104**	**$300**
Operating Expenses				
Wages and Salaries	$37	$37	$37	$37
Depreciation	$1	$1	$1	$1
Other Operating Expenses	$32	$47	$35	$48
EBIT	**$4**	**$4**	**$31**	**$214**
Interest	$3	$3	$3	$3
Taxes	$0	$0	$5	$43
Net	**$1**	**$1**	**$23**	**$168**

Figure 5.11 **Sample Case: Starting Income Statement**

Balance Sheet	
Current Assets	
Cash	$55
Accounts Receivable	$395
Inventory	$805
Other Current Assets	$25
Total Current Assets	**$1,280**
Long-term Assets	$350
Accumulated Depreciation	$50
Total Long-term Assets	**$300**
Total Assets	**$1,580**
Liabilities and Capital	
Current Liabilities	
Accounts Payable	$224
Current Borrowing	$90
Other Current Liabilities	$15
Subtotal Current Liabilities	**$329**
Long-term Liabilities	$285
Total Liabilities	**$614**
Paid-in Capital	$500
Retained Earnings	$418
Earnings	$49
Total Capital	**$967**
Total Liabilities and Capital	**$1,581**
Net Worth	**$967**

Figure 5.12 **Sample Case: Starting Balance**

example of business income, which we'll use as a first step for planning cash. The example already divides sales between cash sales and sales on credit. We also have a simplified version of wages and operating expenses so that we can focus on the cash plan instead of the income statement.

In these two projected statements, the numbers are shown in thousands and may be affected by rounding. You can compare the simplified income statement in Figure 5.11 to the detailed profit and loss example in Figure 5.12.

TIPS & TRAPS

FIXED AND VARIABLE COSTS AND BURN RATE

As you consider your projected income statement, I hope you see three of your spending budgets there—the cost of sales, the payroll, and the expenses. These also contain your fixed vs. variable costs and your burn rate, which I went over in Chapter 4. Those are good numbers to keep in mind.

Why do fixed costs matter? They add to the risk. You have to pay them, whether you're making money or not. Some companies reduce risk by trying to make as much as possible into variable costs, depending on sales, instead of fixed costs. For example, to make programming expenses variable instead of fixed costs, contract the work by milestone, or pay less fixed compensation and more royalty on sales.

The burn rate is the same thing. It's a sense of risk. If you know you need $10,000 every month to cover your burn rate, then when you watch your sales, you have an instant sense of where they have to get.

Calculating the Cash Balance

Cash flow is the change in the balance from one month to another. You calculate cash balance by taking the ending balance from the previous period and adding (or subtracting) cash flow. The sample cash plan in Figure 5.13 does just that.

Calculating cash flow and cash balance isn't always intuitive, but understanding its two main sections is important. (Amounts shown in thousands and may be affected by rounding.)

What you end up with here is a relatively simple cash plan using the direct method to calculate the cash. The direct method means that you add the new sources of cash and subtract the uses of cash, and you have an estimated ending cash balance for each month.

Cash Flow			
Cash Received	Jan	Feb	Mar
Cash from Operations			
Cash Sales	$40	$51	$62
Cash from Receivables	$198	$205	$230
Subtotal Cash from Operations	$238	$256	$293
Additional Cash Received			
New Other Liabilities	$7	$0	$0
New Long-term Liabilities	$0	$0	$100
New Investment Received	$0	$25	$0
Subtotal Cash Received	$245	$281	$393
Expenditures	Jan	Feb	Mar
Expenditures from Operations			
Cash Spending	$47	$47	$47
Bill Payment	$225	$36	$59
Subtotal Spent on Operations	$272	$83	$106
Additional Cash Spent			
Principal Repayment of Current Borrowing	$0	$0	$90
Long-term Liabilities Principal Repayment	$3	$3	$3
Purchase Long-term Assets	$25	$0	$15
Subtotal Cash Spent	$300	$86	$213
Net Cash Flow	($55)	$195	$180
Cash Balance	$1	$196	$376

Figure 5.13 **Calculating the Cash Balance**

Indirect Cash-Flow Method

An alternative cash-flow method, called *indirect*, projects cash flow by starting with net income and adding back depreciation and other noncash expenses, then accounting for the changes in assets and liabilities that aren't recorded in the income statement.

This methodology produces sources and uses of cash statement as shown in Figure 5.14. The results should be identical, for either direct or indirect methods, because the underlying cash flow is identical.

The indirect method starts with net income and then adjusts for all the sources and uses of cash that aren't part of the income

Sources and Uses of Cash (Indirect Cash Flow Method)	Jan	Feb	Mar
Sources of Cash			
Net Income	$1	$1	$23
Depreciation	$1	$1	$1
Increase in Accounts Payable	$0	$14	$241
Decrease in Accounts Receivable	$0	$0	$0
Decrease in Inventory	$185	$243	$46
New Loans	$7	$0	$100
New Investment	$0	$25	$0
Sales Taxes (VAT/GST) Collected	$0	$0	$0
Sale of Assets	$0	$0	$0
Subtotal Sources of Cash	$194	$284	$411
Use of Cash	Jan	Feb	Mar
Decrease in Accounts Payable	$189	$0	$0
Increase in Accounts Receivable	$31	$86	$123
Increase in Inventory	$0	$0	$0
Repay Loans	$3	$3	$93
Purchase Other Assets	$25	$0	$15
Distributions	$0	$0	$0
Sales Tax Payment	$0	$0	$0
Subtotal Uses of Cash	$248	$89	$231
Net Cash Flow	($54)	$195	$180
Cash Balance	$1	$196	$376

Figure 5.14 **Sources and Uses of Cash Statement**

calculation. Results should be the same for either direct or indirect. (Amounts shown in thousands. Numbers may be affected by rounding.)

This finishes up your financial projections, so we can go forward now, and consider the market information people expect in the complete business plan.

Market Research on the Web

For market research, as with business industry research, you go very quickly back to the web. Here are some starting points:

- marketresearch.com—MarketResearch.com is a commercial site aggregating published market research.
- jjhill.org—Hill Research Library, an excellent nonprofit library resource, offers market research at accessible rates.
- business.gov—This is the U.S. government hub site for market research.
- clickz.com/stats—ClickZ Network offers up-to-date statistics on web usage.
- census.gov—The U.S. government's statistical site.
- knowthis.com—KnowThis.com is a marketing information site.
- marketingpower.com—American Marketing Association's (AMA) main market information site.
- hoovers.com—Hoovers is a database of American companies.
- ceoexpress.com—Offers a wealth of links for additional informational sites.
- bea.gov—The Bureau of Economic Analysis is part of the U.S. Department of Commerce, offering business statistics.

Simple and Practical Market Research

Look at existing, similar businesses. This is a very good first step. If you are planning a retail shoe store, for example, spend some time looking at existing retail shoe stores. Park across the street and count the customers who go into the store. Note how long they stay inside and how many come out with boxes that look like purchased shoes. You can probably even count how many pairs of shoes each customer buys. Browse the store and look at prices. Look at several stores, including the discount shoe stores and department store shoe departments.

Find a similar business in another place. If you are planning a local business, find a similar business far enough away that you won't compete. For the shoe store example, you would identify shoe stores in similar towns in other states. Call the owner, explain your purpose truthfully, and ask about the business.

Scan local newspapers for people selling a similar business. Contact the broker and ask for as much information as possible. If you are thinking of creating a shoe store and you find one for sale, you should consider yourself a prospective buyer. Maybe buying the existing store is the best thing. Even if you don't buy, the information you gain will be very valuable. Why is the owner selling? Is there something wrong with the business? You can probably get detailed financial information.

Always shop the competition. If you're in the restaurant business, patronize your competition once a month, rotating through different restaurants. If you own a shoe store, shop your competition once a month, and visit different stores.

If you're considering starting a new business, talk to potential customers.

Talk to Customers

If you're considering starting a new business, talk to potential customers. In the shoe store example, talk to people coming out of existing stores. Talk to your neighbors, talk to your friends, talk to your relatives. Ask them how often they buy shoes, what sizes, where, at what price, and whatever else you can think of. If you're starting a restaurant, landscape architecture business, butcher shop, bakery, or whatever, talk to customers.

At most business schools, when they teach business planning, students have to do a market survey as part of the plan. The plan isn't complete unless they go out and ask a credible number of people what they want, why, where they get it, how much they pay, and so forth. Although you may not go through the formality of a customer survey for your business, this information is vital. At Palo Alto Software, we frequently put a customer survey on two of our websites. People who are browsing the internet looking for materials and information on business plans can visit us at PaloAlto.com or bplans.com.

One of those sites does no selling. Instead, it provides free information, including free downloadable sample plans, outlines, and discussions, including answers to several hundred specific questions about details of developing a business plan. We sometimes ask people stopping by our websites to answer a few quick questions that concern us. The invitation promises just a few questions and promises also that we won't ask for names or e-mail addresses and won't follow up with sales information. When we run one of these surveys, we get about 300 responses a month, which provides us with valuable information about the concerns people have as they consider writing a business plan.

If you have an ongoing business, the process of developing a plan should include talking to customers.

If you have an ongoing business, the process of developing a plan should include talking to customers. Take a step away from the routine, dial up some of your customers, and ask them about your business. How are you doing? Why do they buy? How do they feel about your competitors? It is a good idea to take a customer to lunch once a month, just to keep yourself in touch.

Count Potential Customers

Most business plans contain an analysis of potential customers. As an essential first step, you should have a good idea of how many potential customers there are. The way you find that out depends on your type of business. For example, a retail shoe store needs to know about individuals living in a local area, a graphic design firm needs to know about local businesses, and a national catalog needs to know about households and companies in an entire nation.

What constitutes good sources depends on what you need. Government and commercial statistics are usually more than enough, but for some plans you may end up purchasing information from professional publishers or contract researchers.

> What constitutes good sources depends on what you need.

For general demographic data about a local area, if you have no easier source, ask the reference desk at a local library. A local university library is even better, particularly a business library. Chambers of commerce usually have general information about a local market. In the United States, there is the federal government's U.S. Census Bureau. Nowadays the quickest route to the census bureau is its website at census.gov.

Before the internet became so ubiquitous, I frequently turned to vendors of mailing lists for general information about people and types of businesses. The mailing list vendors often have catalogs listing total numbers of types of people and types of businesses. For example, to find out how many attorneys or CPA offices there are in the United States, I might look at the lists for sale at a list broker.

Magazines provide another good source of demographics. If you're selling to computer stores, for example, call *Computer Retail Week* and *Computer Reseller News* and ask both publications for a media kit. The media kit is intended to sell pages of advertising to potential advertisers. They are frequently full of demographics on the readers. For information on any specific type of business, get the media kits for the magazines that cater to those types of businesses as readers.

Just browsing the Census Bureau website while preparing this book, it took me about 10 minutes to discover that my home county has 378 general contractors, of which 360 have fewer than 20 employees and the remaining 18 have between 20 and 100. There are 238 legal businesses in my county, of which only 12 have more than 20 employees. Also, following the shoe store example, there are 32 shoe stores in the county, none of them having more than 20 employees. There are 111,000 households in the county, 61 percent of them owner occupied, and an average of 2.49 people per household. Some 22 percent of adults in the county are college graduates, and the median household income is $26,000. All of this information was available for free at the census website.

Know Your Customers

Aside from just counting the customers, you also want to know what they need, what they want, and what makes them buy. The more you know about them, the better. For individuals as customers, you probably want to know their average age, income levels, family size, media preferences, buying patterns, and as much else as you can find out that relates to your business. If you can, you want to divide them into groups according to useful classifications, such as income, age, buying habits, social behavior, values, or whatever other factors are important. For the shoe store example, shoe size is good, but you might also want activity preferences and even—if you can find it—psychographics.

The more you know about your customers, the better.

Psychographics divide customers into cultural groups, value groups, social sets, motivator sets, or other interesting categories that might be useful for classifying customers. For example, in literature intended for potential retailers, First Colony Mall of Sugarland, Texas, describes its local area psychographics as including:

- 25 percent kids and cul-de-sacs (upscale suburban families, affluent)
- 5.4 percent winner's circle (suburban executives, wealthy)
- 19.2 percent boomers and babies (young white-collar suburban, upper middle income)
- 7 percent country squires (elite ex-urban, wealthy).

Going into more detail, it calls the kids and cul-de-sacs group "a noisy medley of bikes, dogs, carpools, rock music, and sports." The winner's circle customers are "well-educated, mobile, executives and professionals with teen-aged families. Big producers, prolific spenders, and global travelers." The country squires are "where the wealthy have escaped urban stress to live in rustic luxury. Number four in affluence, big bucks in the boondocks."

Know Your Industry

A standard business plan should explain the general state of the industry and the nature of the business. You might be able to skip this for an internal plan because most of the target readers already know the industry, but even in this case, taking a step away and taking a fresh look can be valuable.

> A standard business plan should explain the general state of the industry and the nature of the business.

Whether you're a service business, manufacturer, retailer, or some other type of business, you should do an industry analysis, describing

- industry participants.
- distribution patterns.
- competition.

There is plenty of information available—too much, in fact; your hardest task is sifting through it all. There are websites for business analysis, financial statistics, demographics, trade associations, and just about everything you'll need for a complete business plan.

Industry Participants

You can't easily describe a type of business without describing the nature of the participants. There is a huge difference, for example, between an industry like long-distance telephone services, in which there are only a few huge companies in any one country, and one like dry cleaning, in which there are tens of thousands of smaller participants.

This can make a big difference to a business and a business plan. The restaurant industry, for example, is what we call *pulverized*, which, like the dry cleaning industry, is made up of many small participants. The fast-food business, on the other hand, is composed of a few national brands participating in thousands of branded outlets, many of them franchised.

The more you know about your customers, the better.

Economists talk of consolidation in an industry as a time when many small participants tend to disappear and a few large players emerge. In accounting, for example, there are a few large international firms whose names are well known and there are tens of thousands of smaller firms. The automobile business is composed of a few national brands participating in thousands of branded dealerships. In computer manufacturing, there are a few large international firms whose names are well known and there are thousands of smaller firms.

Distribution

Explain how distribution works in your industry. Is this an industry in which retailers are supported by regional distributors, as is the case for computer products, magazines, or auto parts? Does this industry depend on direct sales to large industrial customers? Do manufacturers support their own direct sales forces, or do they work with product representatives?

Some products are almost always sold through retail stores to consumers, and sometimes these are distributed by distribution companies that buy from manufacturers. In other cases, the products are sold directly from manufacturers to stores. Some products are sold directly from the manufacturer to the final consumer through mail campaigns, national advertising, the internet, or other promotional means.

In many product categories there are several alternatives, and distribution choices are strategic. Encyclopedias and vacuum cleaners were traditionally sold door-to-door but are now also sold in stores and direct from manufacturer to consumer through radio, television, and Sunday newspaper print ads.

> Technology can change the patterns of distribution in an industry or product category.

Many products are distributed through direct business-to-business sales, in long-term contracts such as the ones between car manufacturers and their suppliers of parts, materials, and components. In some industries companies use representatives, agents, or commissioned salespeople.

Technology can change the patterns of distribution in an industry or product category. The internet, for example, is changing the options for software distribution, books, music, and other products. Cable communication is changing the options for distributing video products and video games.

This topic may not apply to most service companies, because distribution is normally about physical distribution of specific physical products. If you are a restaurant owner, graphic artist, architect, or some other service that doesn't involve distribution, just leave this topic out of your plan.

For a few services, distribution may still be relevant. A phone service, cable provider, or internet provider might describe distribution related to physical infrastructure. Some publishers may prefer to treat their business as a service rather than a manufacturing company, and in that case distribution may also be relevant.

Explain the Sales Forecast

Although the charts and tables are great, you still need to explain them. A complete business plan should normally include some detailed textual discussion of your sales forecast, sales strategy, sales programs, and related information. Ideally, you use the text, tables, and charts in your plan to provide some visual variety and ease of use. Put the tables and charts near the text covering the related topics.

In my standard business plan text outline, the discussion of sales goes into Chapter 5.0, "Strategy and Implementation Summary." You can change that to fit whichever logic and structure you use. In practical terms, you'll probably prepare these text topics as separate items, to be gathered into the plan as it is finished.

Sales Strategy

Somewhere near the sales forecast you should describe your sales strategy. Sales strategies deal with how and when to close sales prospects, how to compensate salespeople, how to optimize order processing and database management, and how to maneuver price, delivery, and conditions.

- How do you sell?
- Do you sell through retail, wholesale, discount, mail order, phone order?
- Do you maintain a sales force?
- How are salespeople trained, and how are they compensated?

Don't confuse sales strategy with your marketing strategy, which goes elsewhere. Sales should close the deals that marketing opens.

To help differentiate between marketing strategy and sales strategy, think of marketing as the broader effort of generating sales leads on a large scale, and sales as the efforts to bring those sales leads into the system as individual sales transactions. Marketing might affect image and awareness and propensity to buy, while sales involves getting the order.

Sales Programs

Details are critical to implementation. Use this topic to list the specific information related to sales programs in your milestones table, with the specific persons responsible, deadlines, and budgets. How is this strategy to be implemented and measured? Do you have concrete and specific plans?

Details are critical to implementation.

Business plans are about results, and generating results depends in part on how specific you are in the plan. For anything related to sales that is supposed to happen, include it here and list the person responsible, dates required, and budgets. All of that will make your business plan more real.

Forecast Details

Your business plan text should summarize and highlight the numbers you have entered in the sales forecast table. Make sure you discuss important assumptions in enough detail and that you explain the background sufficiently. Try to anticipate the questions your readers will ask. Include whatever information you think will be relevant, that your readers will need.

How Many Years?

I believe a business plan should normally project sales by month for the next 12 months and annual sales for the following three years. This doesn't mean businesses shouldn't plan for a longer term than just three years. It does mean, however, that the detail of monthly forecasts doesn't pay off beyond a year, except in special cases. It also means that the detail in the yearly forecasts probably doesn't make sense beyond three years.

It does mean, of course, that you still plan your business for 5, 10, and even 15-year time frames; just don't do it within the detailed context of business plan financials.

Documents, Presentations, Live

One of the principles of the plan-as-you-go business plan is that form follows function. Your plan isn't your plan document. It isn't your elevator speech or your summary memo. Those are outputs.

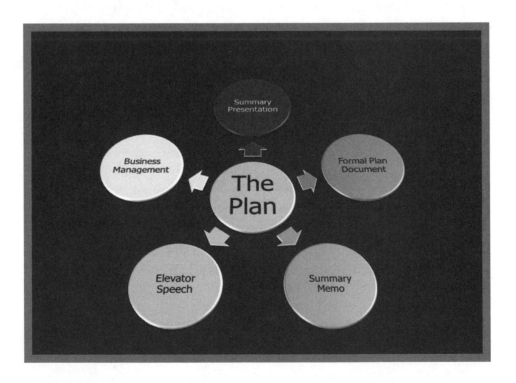

Your plan is what you're going to do with your business. It's what's going to happen, set out concretely so you can track what actually happens and compare it with what you thought would happen.

Think about how the plot of a well-known story generates different versions—the novel, the movie, the television miniseries, the comic book, the performance by the high school drama department. All of them have the same story at their core.

Your business plan is like that, too. What people traditionally think of as the plan, the document, is just an output. Other common outputs include the pitch and the summary.

This matters because people get very confused. "Don't do a business plan," some experts say. "Just do a presentation." They justify that with the idea that few investors read business plans. But wait, the presentation has to describe what you're going to do, so you'd better have a plan. And maybe, just maybe, you don't create the plan document, just the presentation . . . but if so, you'd better know what the plan is.

> *Your plan is what you're going to do with your business.*

In this section I'd like to look at some of the standard outputs: the business plan document, the summary (or summary memo), the elevator speech, and the pitch presentation. For all of these, you start with a plan and then create the output as needed.

And these are hardly the only business plan outputs these days. Others include websites, blogs, and more recently twitter (at twitter.com) had a business plan contest limited to 140 characters. The plan is whatever works for you, but only as long as it works for you.

The Standard Traditional Business Plan

I hope at this point I've made it clear that you don't necessarily need to have a standard, traditional, formal business plan. Until you really need to show a plan to some outsider who needs, wants, or expects the full formal plan, you can just use your plan-as-you-go plan to reap the benefits and avoid the hassle of the document.

However, there are business reasons that force you to produce the traditional plan document. We call these business plan events. The more common business plan events are related to seeking loans or investments. Ironically, the bank loan manager, angel investor, or venture capitalist may not read your plan, but most of them want to know you have one, which means they want it to appear in their inbox or on their desk.

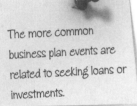

The more common business plan events are related to seeking loans or investments.

Approaching a business plan event without being ready to produce a traditional business plan is something like approaching a publisher without having an outline and sample chapter. You'll look dumb if you don't have it. So have it.

The good news is that you already have the core of your plan ready, so you're a long way down the path from start to done. You have only to dress it up to make it a formal business plan. You know what you want to do, and why, so from here you spin it out from your core into the proper words. You already have the numbers, right? And you know your strategy, too, as well as your dates, deadlines, responsibility assignments, and metrics.

So the bad news is that depending on how much you have, and why you need to show that plan, you may have to go through the exercise of supporting market information with something beyond just hunches and experience. I've said earlier that your plan doesn't necessarily include supporting information like market research and industry analysis, but when you're going to dress it up formally and send it out to represent you, it probably does need to include more background information.

Explanations and Descriptions

As the following table shows, there are lots of sections in the formal plan document that are basically describing and explaining your business to outsiders.

Section	Notes and Comments

1.0 Executive Summary
   1.1 Objectives
   1.2 Mission
   1.3 Keys to Success
	These are pretty much in the *heart of the plan*. I talked about objectives and mission and keys to success in Chapter 3.

2.0 Company Summary
   2.1 Company Ownership
   2.2 Startup Plan (for new companies)
   or Company History (for ongoing companies)
   2.3 Company Locations and Facilities
	The formal plan should include basic summaries to get people up to speed with your company formation, history (if it has a history), locations, facilities, intellectual property, and so on.
	This is where you put your startup costs if you're a startup, or the past performance information if you're an existing and ongoing company.

3.0 Products and Services
   3.1 Product and Service Description
   3.2 Competitive Comparison
   3.3 Sales Literature
   3.4 Sourcing
   3.5 Technology
   3.6 Future Products and Services
	You've gone through this in the heart of the plan, but now we're talking about descriptions and explanations. Keep it simple. Remember, though, that this is a lot about credibility. You're proving that you have an interesting business offering, usually to outsiders. Proof—designs, patents, quotes, and illustrations—is very important. One of the mistakes a lot of people make in a formal business plan document is explaining too much about the technology. A business plan is about the business. Leave the technical explanations for the appendices. Use the team backgrounds and patent information (if you have it) to make the technology credible.

Section	Notes and Comments

4.0 Market Analysis Summary
  4.1 Market Segmentation
  4.2 Target Market Segment Strategy
    4.2.1 Market Needs
    4.2.2 Market Trends
    4.2.3 Market Growth
  4.3 Industry Analysis
    4.3.1 Industry Participants
    4.3.2 Distribution Patterns
    4.3.3 Competition and Buying Patterns
    4.3.4 Main Competitors
	This is mainly the market proof I discussed earlier in this chapter. Write it out, explain it, make it credible, and give it numbers.

5.0 Strategy and Implementation Summary
  5.1 Strategy Pyramids
  5.2 Value Proposition
  5.3 Competitive Edge
  5.4 Marketing Strategy
    5.4.1 Positioning Statements
    5.4.2 Pricing Strategy
    5.4.3 Promotion Strategy
    5.4.4 Distribution Patterns
    5.4.5 Marketing Programs
  5.5 Sales Strategy
    5.5.1 Sales Forecast
    5.5.2 Sales Programs
  5.6 Strategic Alliances
  5.7 Milestones
	You've thought it through. You have the heart of your plan. This is where you explain it in text, preferably in easy-to-read text, full of bullet points.
	
	The good news is that you do know your marketing strategy, sales strategy, and the rest of it. The bad news is that as we get into this as supporting information, you have to take the time to explain and describe it.
	
	The complete plan requires textual explanation of the key numbers and tables you had in your organic plan-as-you-go plan. That includes explaining the assumptions behind the sales forecast, and the business activities in the milestones table. Add simple text with lots of bullets instead of long paragraphs.

Section	Notes and Comments

6.0 Management Summary
   6.1 Organizational Structure
   6.2 Management Team
   6.3 Management Team Gaps
   6.4 Personnel Plan
	For a plan for investment, the description of the management team is often the single most important section. Professional investors usually look to the management team as the best way to reduce risk. They want to see backgrounds, track records, and successes. Angel investors follow the same pattern, and that's also true with business plans for business venture contests. You did a personnel plan in numbers in the expense budgets, and you linked that into the full financial forecast profit and loss. This is where to put that table into the plan.
	The organizational structure is the underlying logic of the who does what part of your plan in flesh and bones. Most standard plans include an organization chart at this point.
	The section on management team gaps build credibility for high-profile plans. If you're taking a plan to investors or to a business plan contest, your readers will probably see those gaps. Don't ignore them. Acknowledge the gaps and show that you're intending to fill them.

7.0 Financial Plan
   7.1 Important Assumptions
   7.2 Key Financial Indicators
   7.3 Break-even Analysis
   7.4 Projected Profit and Loss
   7.5 Projected Cash Flow
	Usually the formal complete plan starts this chapter with a simple summary explanation of the underlying financial strategy. That would be a reference to growing through investment, planning for multiple rounds of investment, for example. Or it could be financing growth with loans, whether SBA guaranteed or not. Or it might

Section	Notes and Comments
7.6 Projected Balance Sheet 7.7 Business Ratios 7.8 Long-Term Plan	be simple bootstrapping (although those businesses aren't as likely to need the formal business plan document). Then most of the rest of this chapter is a matter of showing the financial projections we've discussed in this book. One very important addition, skipped in too many plans, is basic explanations in text. Highlight the growth rates and key points in the tables.

As a general rule, I recommend including just annual projections in the tables embedded in the text of a plan, along with a heavy dose of business charts. Leave the monthly tables for the appendices.

Always Lead with Your Story

Start with stories. In your business plan, your presentation, and even your elevator pitch, always start with a story about who needs what you're selling. Needs and wants are the biggest thing in business, so make them come alive.

Ralph promised his wife, Mabel, that he'd get new suits before his London trip, but Mabel normally goes with him to the stores and she's been busy with their daughter and new grandson, and Ralph hates shopping. His solution, for this and his long-term need for a steady supply of good-looking clothes befitting his position as president and founder of a company, is the Trunk Club. He doesn't have to shop, his clothes will fit, he'll be able to just call the club and ask for what he needs whether it's business casual, office suits, or formal, or even golf and hiking. He'll be in style and matched and he won't have to worry about it. And he won't have to go into a store either.

© En Tien Ou/iStock photo

With apologies to Joanna and Brie, founders of the Trunk Club, I just made that story up to illustrate a point. That one paragraph does a decent job, in my opinion, at setting up the market need, the target market, and the business offering. This is one of the more inter-esting new businesses I've seen lately. The plan, the presentation and the elevator pitch could begin with this story.

Linda's been dreaming about and thinking about the business she wants to start. Sometimes she can't sleep at night for thinking about it. Will people want what I'm selling, she asks herself? How many? How much will they pay? What's the right equipment to start? Can I afford it? What will I need to spend to get going, and what will I need to spend on people, rent, and so on as I start? How much will it cost me to build what I'm delivering? Can I make an offering that will be attractive to outside investors? Finally Linda gets Business Plan Pro and starts working, building the plan. She takes it a topic at a time, a step at a time; she jumps around the different projections and con-cepts. Now when she wakes up in the middle of the night thinking about it, she has a plan under way, somewhere to put those thoughts down. Now she has a much better idea of what she needs, how long it might take, what the key points are.

Leslie and Terry both work, and they also both care very much about creating the right home life for their two children, three and one years old. When they shop for groceries they always go to the more health-oriented grocery store. They buy organic, they cook organic, but they don't always have the time to cook. They hate giving their kids the foods they can get delivered, and they hate giving their kids the meals they can pick up. Then they discover a new business that prepares healthy family meals and sells a subscription plan. Terry stops by several days a week to pick up the family dinner on the way home from work. What business is this story for? You tell me; I'm just thinking here about a problem that needs solving. It's about telling the story. That makes a business plan come alive.

> The more common business plan events are related to seeking loans or investments.

One final example, this one a true story: Recently, I spent most of Thursday and Friday one week at the University of Notre Dame with seven other people reviewing more than 60 executive summaries submitted to the two Notre Dame venture competitions—the McCloskey Business Plan Competition and the newer Sustainable Social Venture Competition. As part of this we reviewed two nearly equal executive summaries. One started with the founder's story of how he had this problem nobody could solve. That one scored significantly higher than the other one, which was relatively similar on all other noticeable points but was missing a story.

This story idea isn't new. For more on how to do it, try reading *Made to Stick* by Chip and Dan Heath, or *All Marketers are Liars* by Seth Godin. What's new here is that I've experienced another example of how much difference this tactic can make. Turn your core marketing strategy into a story, and then tell that story first.

Adapted with permission from Planning Startups Stories blog.

The Executive Summary: Write It for Whoever Will Read It

Let's take a couple of real-world cases. First, the executive summary for a formal business plan, which will be used in a venture competition or as a tool for seeking outside investment. Second, the executive summary for a bank, as part of a loan document. Each of these is a different animal.

A WORD ABOUT WORDS

HEATH BROTHERS ON BUSINESS LANGUAGE

This is where so much business communication goes awry. Mission statements, synergies, strategies, visions—they are often ambiguous to the point of being meaningless. Naturally sticky ideas are full of concrete images . . . because our brains are trained to remember concrete data. In proverbs, abstract truths are often encoded in concrete language. "A bird in the hand is worth two in the bush." Speaking concretely is the only way to ensure that our idea will mean the same thing to everyone in our audience.

Adapted from *Made to Stick* by Chip and Dan Heath.

The Classic: Seeking Investment

This summary, whether you like it or not, performs a sales function. You are selling your concept, your startup, or your growing company to an outsider who is interested in becoming an investor. So put yourself in the investor's place and emphasize the elements that will make her money.

What's strongest about your plan, compared with others? Make that a highlight. You might even lead with it. For example, if you've got a venture already backed by major brand-name investors, say so early in the summary. If you've got a founders team that includes several known entrepreneurs with good track records, then get that upfront. If you have a good business track record, like impressive early sales or landmark deals with major channels or corporations or governments, put that first. If you have an amazing new invention or breakthrough technology, lead with that. Use good judgment. You're an editor, at this point, looking at things through the audience's eyes.

What's strongest about your plan, compared with others?

So the order depends on the specifics of your company, but, regardless of order, here are some elements you should definitely include:

- *The heart of the plan.* That includes the essential reason for buying, the target market, and key elements that match identifiable core competencies and market opportunities.
- *If you have a new product or new technology, sell it to the investors.* Sell it by showing there are already customers and commitments, if you can. If you don't have that, and you have a patent, then say so, but don't think you don't have to defend the patent. Be prepared for objections and don't make the summary imply that a patent alone is enough. If you have working prototypes, say so.
- *Description of the management team.* You can't get away with saying nothing about this. If you have to depend on board members or advisors, so be it; investors are always looking for the team. The better the track record, the lower the risk. If your team has no experience, say very little.
- *Some key numbers.* Usually this includes a sales forecast. In some rare cases, some web companies can get away with forecasting traffic; in those cases, however, they'd better explain a *business model.* Sales are almost always essential, and profits are good too, if you have a realistic projection. Include just a few numbers as bait in the summary; don't go too deep.
- *The offering to investors.* What do you want from investors, and what are you prepared to give in return? You have to see the deal from the investors' point of view. Don't tell them just how great your company will be, tell them how they will make money. They want to know how much money you need now and how much equity you are prepared to give.
- *About the business model: if you have a traditional business, the business model is obvious.* You have to explain it only if it's not

obvious. Channels of distribution can make a big difference too; if your business depends on physical distribution, you should show that you know the channel and that your projections are realistic. Your sales should assume channel margins as well.

The Summary for Lenders

Read through my recommended points for the investment or venture competition-oriented summary, and think about the revisions you'll want for a summary for a bank. Here are some highlights you want to hit:

- *The heart of the plan*. Just about the same as for investors. People want to know what you're doing.
- *Financial history*. How long have you been in business? What legal formation or legal entity is involved? Who owns this company, and what kind of financial history does he have?
- *A balance sheet*. Banks can't lend you money for ideas; they need to secure the money with assets. You have to have more assets than liabilities.

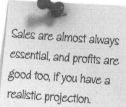

Sales are almost always essential, and profits are good too, if you have a realistic projection.

- *Payment history*. Your company has to live with the debt and payment record it has, and the bank has to check that. Give it a head start.
- *Description of the management team*. You can't get away with saying nothing about this. If you have to depend on board members or advisors, so be it; investors are always looking for the team. The better the track record, the less the risk. If your team has no experience, say very little.
- *Some key numbers*. Usually this includes a sales forecast. In some rare cases, some web companies can get away with forecasting traffic; in those cases, however, they'd better explain a *business model*. Sales are almost always essential, and profits are good too, if you have a realistic projection. Include just a

few numbers to make your reader interested in the summary; don't go too deep.

■ *For bank purposes, expect to submit a complete financial projection* including profit and loss, balance sheet, and cash flow, both for recent past and future projections.

What Else Should an Executive Summary Include?

For a standard summary you should generally include:

■ business name
■ business location
■ what product or service you sell
■ purpose of the plan

Another paragraph should highlight important points, such as projected sales and profits, unit sales, profitability, and keys to success. Include the news you don't want anyone to miss. This is a good place to put a highlights chart, a bar chart that shows sales, gross margin, and profits before interest and taxes for the next three years. You should also cite and explain those numbers in the text.

How Long Should an Executive Summary Be?

The shorter, the better. If you can say it in a single page, then wow, that's really impressive. Generally two pages is better than five, and five is better than ten, but ten pages is probably too much.

Stay sensitive to the exact purpose and audience. These days you run into situations in which people use the phrase "executive summary" to mean "business plan, but keep it short." Always ask what people are looking for specifically, if you can.

Particularly in venture competitions, find out what the general standard is and how the summary will be used. I've seen competitions (and been among the judges as well)

Always ask what people are looking for specifically, if you can.

in which the best summaries were penalized for being short. Longer summaries seemed to do better because they included more information and the judges were impressed. The short ones didn't get a chance to make all the points they wanted.

Realize that some people say summary or summary memo when what they want is a one-page letter or e-mail. As I said earlier, always ask if you can.

If you check around, you'll see that experts differ on how long an executive summary or summary memo should be. Some insist that it takes just a page or two, others recommend a more detailed summary, taking as much as ten pages, covering enough information to substitute for the plan itself. Although business plans of more than 50 pages used to be common, investors and lenders these days expect a concise, focused plan.

The Pitch Presentation

For a bit of venture capital history, the pitch presentation became fashionable in the late 1990s during the dotcom boom, when

investors were frequently buying into businesses that had website traffic and no money, and no business model they could use to get money.

The pitch presentation is a 20-minute (or so) slide presentation, usually done live but with either PowerPoint or Keynote slides in the background, that tells investors about a new business.

The best writing anywhere on this is in Guy Kawasaki's "Art of the Pitch" chapter in his book *The Art of the Start*.

I'm happy to say that Kawasaki has posted much of the same material on his

THE ART OF THE START

by Guy Kawasaki

blog, in the post named "The 10/20/30 Rule for PowerPoint Presentations." He says on that post:

> *It's quite simple: a PowerPoint presentation should have ten slides, last no more than twenty minutes, and contain no font smaller than thirty points. While I'm in the venture capital business, this rule is applicable for any presentation to reach agreement: for example, raising capital, making a sale, forming a partnership, etc.*
>
> *Ten is the optimal number of slides in a PowerPoint presentation because a normal human being cannot comprehend more than ten concepts in a meeting—and venture capitalists are very normal. (The only difference between you and a venture capitalist is that he is getting paid to gamble with someone else's money.) If you must use more than ten slides to explain your business, you probably don't have a business. The ten topics that a venture capitalist cares about are:*

1. *Problem*
2. *Your solution*
3. *Business model*
4. *Underlying magic/technology*
5. *Marketing and sales*
6. *Competition*
7. *Team*
8. *Projections and milestones*
9. *Status and timeline*
10. *Summary and call to action*

Of course that's an excellent general guideline, but you'll customize and tailor it to fit your exact needs.

For example, you don't need a slide on the business model unless your model is unusual. If you're buying things and reselling them with a profit margin, or you're providing a service and making a profit, or manufacturing something that you can sell for a profit, then ignore the business model. If it isn't obvious, then you have to explain it. That comes up most often with website businesses.

Or, if you're doing a presentation for your own team, summarizing the key points in your business plan, you don't necessarily include slides showing the team, or the business model, or the underlying magic. Those descriptions are for outsiders, not for internal use.

Always be flexible. Don't change the truth for a presentation, but do present first that part of the truth that answers the audience's most important questions. Make the presentation easy for people to follow, and highlight the most important things, not all the details.

Please use good presentation technique. Give people pictures to look at that are related to your topic, but not lots of bullet points to read while you talk.

PowerPoint slide presentations can be terribly boring. Read Garr Reynolds's book *Presentation Zen* if you can, or Cliff Atkinson's book *Beyond Bullet Points*, or Seth Godin's excellent post "Really Bad PowerPoint," on his blog at sethgodin.type pad.com or, at the very least, Guy Kawasaki's chapter on presentations in *The Art of the Start*.

Don't forget that you might be using a slide presentation as the only output of

PRESENTATION ZEN
by Garr Reynolds

BEYOND BULLET POINTS
by Cliff Atkinson

your core business plan. That would be unusual, but it could work very well. Instead of bullet points or an elevator speech, wrap it up in a slide presentation. Then you'll be ready when the pitch moment comes.

The Summary Memo

The summary memo is a separate document, usually just a few pages, that describes your business plan. It comes up sometimes when you're dealing with outsiders. For example, if you're looking for investment, someone might respond to a short elevator speech with "Send me the summary memo."

> The summary memo is a separate document, usually just a few pages, that describes your business plan.

Some experts will talk as if this were a set format, entirely according to a recipe, but it isn't. It depends a whole lot on who wants it. Some investors want a two- to five-page document, ideally in PDF format attached to an e-mail. Some venture contests want five to ten pages, with specific contents from some list. Some people are talking about a few paragraphs in a letter or an e-mail.

When a plan is used to back up a loan application or to explain a business to potential investors, it may require a special summary document as well as a complete plan. Many investors like to see a brief summary, and a loan application doesn't always require a complete plan. If you develop your plan in the right way, you can use the summary paragraphs of the main sections—company, market, product—to create these summary documents.

Writing a Summary

Remember, form follows function. The executive summary and the summary memo might be two different items, the executive summary that appears as the first chapter of your business plan, in the long plan document and the summary memo, which is a stand-alone document you use to summarize your plan to outsiders who don't want to read the whole plan.

Sometimes, however, for practical reasons, you can work with a single item. The same summary that you print at the beginning of your plan can also stand alone as a summary memo. Use depends on what you need and who's asking.

In either case, the summary is going to work around the heart of your plan, the core strategy: what you're offering to whom, what's different about you, and your strategic focus. However, you should tailor that to address the specific purpose of your summary, meaning who's going to read it, which should tell you what points to emphasize.

And it is a summary of the highlights of your business plan. Even though the topic appears first in the printed document, most business plan developers leave the writing of the executive summary until the end. This summary is the doorway to the rest of the plan; get it right or your target readers will not go further.

The truth is always the truth. It doesn't change when the audience changes. What does change, however, is what shows up with emphasis and what becomes less important.

The Elevator Speech

If you can't give your elevator speech in 60 seconds, you have a problem. Your strategy isn't clear enough. It should be a quick description of the business that you could give in the time you share with a stranger in an elevator. The term is becoming popular in the everyday language of the entrepreneur, the venture capitalist, and the teaching of

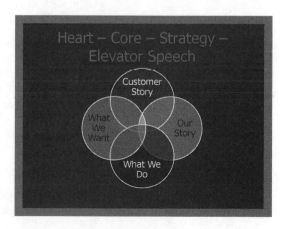

entrepreneurship. There are even elevator speech contests at business schools.

I don't think it's academic, though. I think it's important. I think it's a great exercise that everybody in business should be able to do. Let's get simple, let's get focused, let's get powerful. So we're talking about the heart of the plan strategy. What better way to condense it than in a quick elevator speech? If you can't do it, worry.

Start with a Story

Once again, start your speech with a person (or business or organization) in a situation. Personalize. Identify clearly. For example:

John Jones doesn't particularly care about clothes, but he knows he has to look good. He sees clients every day in the office, and he lives in a ritzy suburb, where he often sees clients by accident on weekends. But he hates to shop for clothes. (The Trunk Club)

Jane Smith wants to do her own business plan. She knows her business and what she wants to do, but wants help organizing the plan and getting the right pieces together. The plan needs to look professional because she's promised to show it to her bank as part of the merchant account process. (Business Plan Pro)

Acme Consulting has five people managing three shared e-mail addresses: info@acme.com, sales@acme.com, and admin@acme.com. The five of them have trouble not stepping on each other. Sometimes a single e-mail gets answered three or four times, with different answers. Sometimes an e-mail goes unanswered for days, because everybody thinks somebody else answered it. (EmailCenter Pro)

Notice that in each of these examples I could be much more general. The Trunk Club targets mainly men who don't like to shop but need to dress well and have enough money to pay for a shopping service. Business Plan Pro is for the do-it-yourselfer who wants good business planning software. EmailCenter Pro is for companies managing shared e-mail addresses like sales@ or info@. But instead of generally describing a market, I've made it personal.

Sometimes you can get away with generalizing. "Farmers in the Willamette Valley," for example, or "parents of gifted children." It's an easy way to slide into describing a market. However, I suspect that you're almost always better off starting with a more readily imaginable single person, and let that person stand for your target market.

Follow with What's Special About You

In the next part of your elevator speech, address "Why you"? Why your business? What's special about you that makes your offering or solution interesting to the target person or organization you just identified?

This is where you bring in your background, your core competence, your track record, your management team, or whatever. For example:

> *The Trunk Club invented the best-possible solution to this problem. Founder Joanna Van Vleck first succeeded in sales at Nordstrom and then took her personalized shopping-for-other styles into a hugely successful first market in Bend, Oregon. Now, having proven the idea on the front lines . . .*

> *Palo Alto Software has dedicated itself to business planning for more than 20 years. Its founder is one of the best-known experts in the field. Its current management team grew up with business planning, in the trenches. The 8-person development team has more than 50 person years in the same focused area.*

> *Palo Alto Software has been managing this e-mail problem internally for more than ten years now, and has been working with its own inhouse solution for nine years. It has a very strong relationship with hundreds of thousands of small but growing businesses.*

Make sure your point is the right point: benefits to the target customer.

What we focus on here is core competence and differentiation. And, in the classic elevator speech, you have to say it fast. You make your point quickly and go on.

Make sure your point is the right point: benefits to the target customer. It's not what's great about you, but rather whatever lends credibility to your ability to meet the need and solve the problem.

I included two different paragraphs for the same company on purpose. See how the unique qualifications differ for different contexts. It's the same company, but in the first example, the speech is relating to Business Plan Pro, the flagship product. In the second example, the speech is building up EmailCenter Pro, the new product. The descriptions have to change for each.

You might also think of this as the classic "What do you bring to the party?" question. It's not just your brilliance or good looks or great track record, it's fostering credibility for solving the problem.

Then Explain Your Offering

Now explain what that customer you're selling to gets. You've personalized the need or want, identified your unique qualities to solve the problem, and now you have to put the need or want in concrete terms that anybody can see. For example:

> *For a Trunk Club member, when his wife says it's time for a new trip or a new activity is coming up, or the mood strikes him, he just grabs the phone and calls his Trunk Club counselor. "I need more casual stuff for the golf course, or cargo pants for hiking, or two more slack-and-sports-coat combinations." She knows his size, knows what he likes, what his wife likes, and what he needs. The new clothes come three days later, with a complete money-back guarantee if he or his wife doesn't like them.*

> *Business Plan Pro lets Jane jump into and out of her business plan at a moment's notice whenever she wants. She can start with*

the core strategy and build it in blocks, planning while she goes, refining projections as needed. It's built around a solid, error-checked, financially and mathematically correct financial model, and a generalized set of suggestions for outlines, but is also completely flexible for adding and deleting topics and creating a unique business plan. Each task, whether topic or table, comes with easy-to-understand instructions and useful examples.

EmailCenter Pro lets a team share an e-mail address like sales@ or info@ efficiently. E-mails can be assigned to team members or not, and answered e-mails are processed and visible, unanswered e-mails remain at the top until answered. Furthermore, it manages collections of snippets or text templates to build on standard but flexibly customizable answers to frequently asked questions.

In each example here, we can see clearly how this product or service meets the need or solves the problem. Forget features as much as possible, and illustrate benefits. You've already described the person with the problem, and built up your ability to solve it, so now it's just about the solution. Stay focused and concentrated. People will get one or at the most two unique attributes of your business offering. Don't confuse them with more.

People will get one or at the most two unique attributes of your business offering.

A Note about Context

For the purposes of planning as you go, that's it, you've done your elevator speech. However, since we're right here together on this page at the end of this discussion, let me suggest what you might do in a real elevator speech situation: finish strong. The finish depends on who you are, where you are, and what you want. If you've personalized in the first part, sold yourself and/or your organization in the second, and established the attractiveness or suitability of the business offering in the third, it's time to finish strong with a closing.

Your closing depends completely on context. What do you want from the person or people you're talking to? The classic elevator speech context is a venture competition when looking for investors. But there's also the true elevator speech for the established company, simply describing your company to somebody who asked, with no real close. Be honest, you're not always asking for an order, even when you're just chatting with the person in the next seat on the plane. If you are trying to sell, then do ask for the order. Seriously: "If you give me a card, I'll send you a copy with an invoice. If you don't like it, send it back. Here's my card."

> *What do you want from the person or people you're talking to?*

For the venture competition or investment-variety elevator speech, don't try to convey too much information. Do establish in general terms where you are or what you want. "We're looking for seed money of half a million dollars." Or "We're now raising round two financing of three million dollars to be used for the mainstream marketing launch." Or "We're looking for serious marketing partners able to put money upfront in return for privileged first-year pricing." Or "We're trying to establish a royalty relationship with an appropriate manufacturer." And then, ask for a business card, and give one. "If you know anybody who might fit that bill, feel free to recommend us." Or "please give me a call." Don't offer to send a business plan, and don't ask a person directly to invest when it's about investment; reduce the awkwardness by suggesting that your audience might know somebody, not that your audience might invest.

Don't talk terms in the elevator speech. Just establish what you want or need.

If you're in a real elevator with a real potential investor, soft pedal: "If you know anybody who might be interested, please pass this along. Or maybe you want a business card and a follow-up e-mail."

And if you're doing an elevator speech in a business venture competition, close with an appropriate call for investment. Venture competitions always hinge on the would-be or hypothetical pitch to the investor, so make it clear. The better ones end up with something like an intriguing reference to seed capital or first-round equity investment. Stay general. Make them want more.

Planning Process

Throughout this book, I've been reinforcing as much as I could that it's about planning, not the plan. In this chapter, I want to gather all the pieces together and drive that point home.

This chapter is about planning as management.

Item	Description
A Plan vs. Actual Analysis	It's not just accounting, or the technical term *variance*. It's about the management that results from it.
Management and Accountability	It doesn't happen automatically. Accountability is a matter of setting the right metrics and tracking performance. This should be part of the planning process.
Crystal Ball and Chain	Realize that some people fear metrics and planning as something that will be used against them in the future. Avoid this problem by making sure it's collaborative.
Set Expectations and Follow Up	The secret of management is setting expectations and following up with reviews of performance. This is part of your planning process.

A Plan vs. Actual Analysis

Let's look at a simple example of how plan vs. actual analysis works.

For the record, in accounting and financial analysis, they call the difference between plan and actual *variance*. It's a good word to know. Furthermore, you can have positive or negative variance, as in good variance and bad variance.

Positive Variance

- It comes out as a positive number.
- If you sell more than planned, that's good. If profits are higher than planned, that's good too. So for sales and profits, variance is actual results less planned results (subtract plan from actual).

■ For costs and expenses, spending less than planned is good, so positive variance is when the actual amount is less than the planned amount. To calculate subtract actual costs (or expenses) from planned costs.

Negative Variance

■ The opposite. When sales or profits are less than planned, that's bad. You calculate variance on sales and profits by subtracting plan from actual.

■ When costs or expenses are more than planned, that's also bad. Once again, you subtract actual results from the planned results.

I'd like to show you this with a simple example. Let's start with a beginning sales plan, then look at variance and explore what it means. We'll work with a simple sales forecast table—a portion, showing just three months— from a standard sales forecast.

To set the scene, Figure 6.1 shows the sales forecast as the business plan is finished.

Figure 6.2 shows the actual results for the same company for the first three months of the plan.

The numbers at the end of March show actual sales numbers plus adjustments and course corrections.

	Jan	Feb	Mar
Unit Sales			
Systems	85	115	145
Service	200	200	200
Software	150	200	250
Training	145	155	165
Other	160	176	192
Total Unit Sales	740	846	952
Unit Prices	Jan	Feb	Mar
Systems	$2,000	$2,000	$2,000
Service	$75	$69	$58
Software	$200	$200	$200
Training	$37	$35	$39
Other	$300	$300	$300
Sales			
Systems	$170,000	$230,000	$290,000
Service	$15,000	$13,800	$11,600
Software	$30,000	$40,000	$50,000
Training	$5,365	$5,425	$6,435
Other	$48,000	$52,800	$57,600
Total Sales	$268,365	$342,025	$415,635
1st Year Planned	1st Year Actual		1st Year Variance

Figure 6.1 **Beginning Sales Plan**

	Jan	Feb	Mar
Unit Sales			
Systems	63	74	108
Service	168	171	174
Software	174	235	289
Training	156	171	183
Other	162	151	220
Total Unit Sales	723	802	974
Unit Prices	Jan	Feb	Mar
Systems	$1,783	$1,801	$1,791
Service	$103	$106	$88
Software	$224	$185	$277
Training	$48	$39	$46
Other	$291	$371	$222
Sales			
Systems	$112,329	$133,274	$193,428
Service	$17,304	$18,126	$15,312
Software	$38,976	$43,475	$80,053
Training	$7,488	$6,669	$8,418
Other	$47,142	$56,021	$48,840
Total Sales	$223,239	$257,565	$346,051
1st Year Planned	1st Year Actual	1st Year Variance	

Figure 6.2 **Actual Sales Results**

So the calculations are simple enough. You calculate the variance in sales by subtracting the planned amount from the actual amount, which gives us the table shown in Figure 6.3.

I use the classic accountant's red to indicate negative numbers, as in the phrase "in the red." The negatives are also in parentheses. For those cases, the actual sales were lower than planned. Positive numbers here mean actual sales were higher than planned.

You probably see some obvious conclusions. These are just numbers, but they also indicate areas that call for more management.

1. The negative results for unit sales of systems are well below plan. And the per-unit revenue is down too.

	Jan	Feb	Mar
Unit Sales			
Systems	(22)	(41)	(37)
Service	(32)	(29)	(26)
Software	24	35	39
Training	11	16	18
Other	2	(25)	28
Total Unit Sales	(17)	(44)	22
Unit Prices	Jan	Feb	Mar
Systems	($217.00)	($199.00)	($209.00)
Service	$28.00	$37.00	$30.00
Software	$24.00	($15.00)	$77.00
Training	$11.00	$4.00	$7.00
Other	($9.00)	$71.00	($78.00)
Sales			
Systems	($57,671)	($96,726)	($96,572)
Service	$2,304	$4,326	$3,712
Software	$8,976	$3,475	$30,053
Training	$2,123	$1,244	$1,983
Other	($858)	$3,221	($8,760)
Total Sales	($45,126)	($84,460)	($69,584)
1st Year Planned	1st Year Actual	1st Year Variance	

Figure 6.3 **Plan vs. Actual Sales (Variance)**

2. Although units of service are disappointing, the price per unit was up, so sales were above plan.
3. There were pleasant surprises as well for software and training.

Adjusting the Sales Plan

Given what's happened with the sales results, the plan-as-you-go planning process indicates in this example that systems sales are going badly, but there are other sales that can make up the difference.

Do you change the plan? That's where the management comes in. Get your people together and talk about it. Why are systems sales so much less than planned? Were the assumptions wrong?

PARADOX: CONSISTENCY VS. THE BRICK WALL

One of the more stubborn recurrent paradoxes in all business planning is the problem of consistency vs. the brick wall.

Consistency refers to a fact of life in small-business strategy: it's better to have a mediocre strategy consistently applied over three or more years than a series of brilliant strategies, each applied for six months or so. This is frustrating, because people get bored with consistency, and almost always the people running a strategy are bored with it long before the market understands it.

For example, I was consulting with Apple Computer during the 1980s when the Macintosh platform became the foundation of what we now call desktop publishing. We take it for granted today, but back in 1985 when the first laser printers came out, it was like magic. Suddenly a single person in a home office could produce documents that looked professional.

People might argue with this, but what I think I saw in Apple at that time was smart young managers getting bored with desktop publishing long before the market even understood what it was. They started looking at multimedia and other bright, shiny new things, lost concentration on desktop publishing, and lost a lot of market potential as Windows vendors moved in with competitive products.

The brick wall, on the other hand, refers to the futility of trying to implement a flawed plan. You've probably run into this problem at times. People insist on doing something "because that's the plan" when in fact it just isn't working. That kind of thinking has something to do with why some web companies survived the first dotcom boom and others didn't. It also explains why some business experts question the value of the business plan. That's sloppy thinking, in my opinion, confusing the value of the planning with the mistake of implementing a plan without change or review, just because it's the plan.

This consistency vs. revision paradox is one of the best and most obvious reasons for having people—owners and managers—run the business planning, rather than algorithms or artificial intelligence. It takes people to deal with this critical judgment.

PARADOX: CONSISTENCY VS. THE BRICK WALL, CONTINUED

One good way to deal with it is focusing on the assumptions. Identify the key assumptions and whether or not they've changed. When assumptions have changed, there is no virtue whatsoever in sticking to the plan you built on top of them. Use your common sense. Were you wrong about the whole thing or just about timing? Has something else happened, like market problems or disruptive technology, or competition, to change your basic assumptions?

Do not revise your plan glibly. Remember that some of the best strategies take longer to implement. Remember also that you're living with it every day; it is naturally going to seem old to you, and boring, long before the target audience gets it.

Was the plan too optimistic? Has something happened—new competition, for example, or new technology, or something else—to change the situation?

What about the people? Here's where you have to manage expectations and follow up. Do you have metrics on sales presentations, leads, close rates? Have the people been performing, but just not getting the sales? Was your pipeline assumption wrong?

For this example, let's say we decide to adjust the sales forecast to absorb some changed assumptions. Figure 6.4 shows the new sales forecast, after adjustments.

The illustration shows the revised plan in the April and May columns, even before they happen, to reflect the changes shown in the January–March period. Why would we work with an obsolete plan when the situation has changed.

Does this blow the plan vs. actual comparisons for future months? Not if you make the changes correctly, with everybody on the team being aware of them. You just keep moving your plan forward into time, revising for future months.

	Jan	Feb	Mar	Apr	May
Unit Sales					
Systems	63	74	108	150	200
Service	168	171	174	175	255
Software	174	235	289	375	450
Training	156	171	183	200	250
Other	162	151	220	240	200
Total Unit Sales	723	802	974	1,140	1,355
Unit Prices	Jan	Feb	Mar	Apr	May
Systems	$1,783	$1,801	$1,791	$1,775	$1,775
Service	$103	$106	$88	$90	$90
Software	$224	$185	$277	$275	$275
Training	$48	$39	$46	$50	$50
Other	$291	$371	$222	$300	$150
Sales					
Systems	$112,329	$133,274	$193,428	$266,250	$355,000
Service	$17,304	$18,126	$15,312	$15,750	$22,950
Software	$38,976	$43,475	$80,053	$103,125	$123,750
Training	$7,488	$6,669	$8,418	$10,000	$12,500
Other	$47,142	$56,021	$48,840	$72,000	$30,000
Total Sales	$223,239	$257,565	$346,051	$467,125	$544,200
1st Year Planned		1st Year Actual		1st Year Variance	

Figure 6.4 **Adjusted Sales Forecast**

In the end, it's not a game. So what if you change the scoring in the middle? The point is managing the company better. Since the company knows systems sales would be down, it has planned on it and made a revised forecast in the actuals area. The same revision affects projected profits, balance sheet, and, most important, cash.

Starting Plan for Profit and Loss

Following the previews sales example, the planned profit and loss table in Figure 6.5 shows a portion of the profit and loss for the sample company, as it stood in the original plan.

	Jan	Feb	Mar
Sales	$268,365	$342,025	$415,635
Direct Costs of Goods	$184,510	$243,061	$301,612
Fulfillment Payroll	$9,500	$9,500	$9,500
Other	$500	$500	$500
Cost of Goods Sold	$194,510	$253,061	$311,612
Gross Margin	$73,856	$88,965	$104,024
Gross Margin %	27.52%	26.01%	25.03%
Operating Expenses			
Sales and Marketing Expenses			
Sales and Marketing Payroll	$24,000	$24,000	$24,000
Ads	$5,000	$5,000	$7,000
Catalog	$2,000	$3,000	$2,000
Mailing	$3,000	$11,800	$5,500
Promo	$0	$0	$0
Shows	$0	$0	$0
Literature	$0	$7,000	$0
PR	$0	$0	$0
Seminar	$1,000	$0	$0
Service	$2,000	$1,000	$1,000
Training	$450	$450	$450
Total Sales and Marketing Expenses	$37,450	$52,250	$39,950
Sales and Marketing %	13.95%	15.28%	9.61%
1st Year Planned	1st Year Actual	1st Year Variance	

Figure 6.5 **Planned Profit and Loss**

This table shows the gross margin and sales and marketing expense area of the original plan. This is a portion of the full table.

Actual Results for Profit and Loss

Figure 6.6 shows the actual results recorded in that portion of the profit and loss, after the end of March. The actual results mean little without comparison with the original profit and loss table (Figure 6.5). Unfortunately, many businesses also forget to compare the original plan with the actual results. Especially if business is going well—the operation shows a profit, and cash flow is satisfactory—comparisons with the original budget are made poorly or not at all.

This table shows actual results. Note how actual sales, costs, and expenses are different from the *planned numbers*. This is a portion of the full table.

	Jan	Feb	Mar
Sales	$223,239	$257,565	$346,051
Direct Costs of Goods	$141,394	$176,275	$240,051
Fulfillment Payroll	$9,308	$9,224	$9,759
Other	$33	$782	$436
Cost of Goods Sold	$150,735	$186,281	$250,246
Gross Margin	$72,504	$71,284	$95,805
Gross Margin %	32.48%	27.68%	27.69%
Operating Expenses			
Sales and Marketing Expenses			
Sales and Marketing Payroll	$23,456	$24,529	$23,871
Ads	$0	$22,674	$7,896
Catalog	$2,200	$3,100	$2,095
Mailing	$1,873	$12,075	$6,621
Promo	$0	$0	$0
Shows	$0	$0	$0
Literature	$0	$0	$6,401
PR	$0	$0	$0
Seminar	$1,000	$0	$0
Service	$0	$3,023	$1,023
Training	$0	$1,000	$500
Total Sales and Marketing Expenses	$28,529	$66,401	$48,407
Sales and Marketing %	12.78%	25.78%	13.99%
1st Year Planned	1st Year Actual	1st Year Variance	

Figure 6.6 **Actual Results for Profit and Loss**

Profit and Loss Variance

The illustration in Figure 6.7 shows the variance in expenses. The actual results are subtracted from the budget numbers, leaving negative numbers when the actual spending was more than budgeted or when the sales or profits were less than budgeted. Variances are calculated differently in different portions of the plan.

- In expense rows, variance becomes the planned amount minus the actual amount. Lower expenses are a positive variance.
- In the profits and sales areas, variance becomes actual amount minus planned amount. In these cases, higher sales are a positive variance.

The illustration shows a portion of the profit and loss variance table. March results showed sales below plan and costs also below

	Jan	Feb	Mar
Sales	($45,126)	($84,460)	($69,584)
Direct Costs of Goods	$43,116	$66,786	$61,561
Fulfillment Payroll	$192	$276	($259)
Other	$467	($282)	$64
Cost of Goods Sold	$43,775	$66,780	$61,366
Gross Margin	($1,352)	($17,681)	($8,219)
Gross Margin %	4.96%	1.67%	2.66%
Operating Expenses			
Sales and Marketing Expenses			
Sales and Marketing Payroll	$544	($529)	$129
Ads	$5,000	($17,674)	($896)
Catalog	($200)	($100)	($95)
Mailing	$1,127	($275)	($1,121)
Promo	$0	$0	$0
Shows	$0	$0	$0
Literature	$0	$7,000	($6,401)
PR	$0	$0	$0
Seminar	$0	$0	$0
Service	$2,000	($2,023)	($23)
Training	$450	($550)	($50)
Total Sales and Marketing Expenses	$8,921	($14,151)	($8,457)
Sales and Marketing %	1.18%	-10.50%	-4.38%
1st Year Planned	1st Year Actual	1st Year Variance	

Figure 6.7 **Plan vs. Actual Profit and Loss (Variance)**

plan, for a negative variance in sales and a positive variance in cost of goods sold. The result is a smaller negative variance in gross margin.

Understanding Variance Analysis

Many businesses, especially the small, entrepreneurial kind, ignore or forget the other half of the budgeting. Budgets are too often proposed, discussed, accepted, and forgotten. Variance analysis looks after the fact at what caused a difference between plan and actual numbers. Good management looks at what that difference means to the business.

Variance analysis ranges from simple and straightforward to sophisticated and complex. Some cost-accounting systems separate variances into many types and categories. Sometimes a single result can be broken down into many different variances, both positive and negative.

The most sophisticated systems separate unit and price factors on materials, hours worked, cost per hour on direct labor, and fixed and variable overhead variances. Though difficult, this kind of analysis can be invaluable in a complex business.

Look for Specifics

This presentation of variances shows how important good analysis is. In theory, the positive variances are good news because they mean spending was less than budgeted. The negative variance means spending was more than the budget.

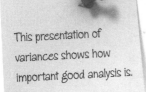

This presentation of variances shows how important good analysis is.

Continuing with our example, the $5,000 positive variance in advertising in January means $5,000 less than planned was spent, and the $7,000 positive variance for literature in February means $7,000 less than planned was spent. The negative variance for advertising in February and March and the negative variance for literature in March show that more was spent than was planned for those items.

Evaluating these variances takes thought. Positive variances aren't always good news. For example:

■ The positive variance of $5,000 in advertising means that money wasn't spent, but it also means that advertising wasn't placed. Systems sales were way below expectations for this same period—could the advertising missed in January be a possible cause?

■ For literature, the positive $7,000 in February may be evidence of a missed deadline for literature that wasn't actually completed until March. If so, at least it appears that the costs on completion were $6,401, a bit less than the $7,000 planned.

Among the larger single variances for an expense item in a month shown in the illustration was the positive $7,000 variance for the new literature expenses in February. Is this good news or bad news? Every variance should stimulate questions.

- Why did one project cost more or less than planned?
- Were objectives met?
- Does a positive variance reflect a cost saving or a failure to implement?
- Does a negative variance reflect a change in plans, a management failure, or an unrealistic budget?

A variance table can provide management with significant information. Without this data, some of these important questions might go unasked.

More on Variance

Variance analysis on sales can be very complex. There can be significant differences between projected and actual sales because of different unit volumes or because of different average prices. In the sales variance example in this chapter, the units variance shows that the sales of systems were disappointing. In the expenses variance, however, we can see that advertising and mailing costs were below plan. Could there be a correlation between the saved expenses in mailing and the lower-than-planned sales? Yes, of course there could.

The mailing cost was much less than planned, but as a result the planned sales never came. The positive expense variance is thus not good for the company. Sales and marketing expenses were also above plan in March, causing another negative variance.

Variance analysis on sales can be very complex.

The sales forecast variance table (Figure 6.3), which compares units variance and sales variance, yields no surprises.

The lower-than-expected unit sales also had lower-than-expected sales values. Compare that with service, in which lower units yielded higher sales (indicating much higher prices than planned). Is this an indication of a new profit opportunity or a new trend? This clearly depends on the specifics of your business.

It is often hard to tell what caused differences in costs. If spending schedules aren't met, variance might be caused simply by lower unit volume. Management probably wants to know the results per unit, and the actual price, and the detailed feedback on the marketing programs.

Summary

The quality of a business plan is measured not by the quality of its ideas, analysis, or presentation, but only by the implementation it causes. It is true, of course, that some business plans are developed only as selling documents to generate financial resources. For these plans, their worth is measured by their effectiveness in selling a business opportunity to a prospective investor. For plans created to help run a business, their worth is measured by how much they help run a business—in other words, their implementation.

Variance analysis is vital to good management. You have to track and follow up on budgets, mainly through variance analysis, or the budgets will be useless.

Although variance analysis can be very complex, the main guide is common sense. In general, going under budget is a positive variance, and going over budget is a negative variance. But the real test of management should be whether or not the result was good for business.

Variance analysis is vital to good management.

Management and Accountability

Every small-business owner suffers the problem of management and accountability. It's much easier to be friends with the people you work with than to manage them well.

Correct management means setting expectations well and then following up on results. Compare results with expectations. People on a team are held accountable only if management actually does the work of tracking results and communicating results, after the fact, to the people responsible.

Metrics are part of the problem. As a rule we don't develop the right metrics for people. Metrics aren't right unless the people responsible understand them and believe in them. Will the measurement scheme show good performances and bad performances?

The metrics should be built into the plan. Remember, people need metrics. People want metrics.

Then you have to track. That's where the plan-as-you-go business plan creates a management advantage, because tracking and following up is part of its most important pieces. Set the review schedules in advance, make sure you have the right participants for the review, and then do it.

In good teams, the negative feedback is in the metrics. Nobody has to scold or lecture, because the team participated in generating the plan and the team reviews it, and good performances make people proud and happy, and bad performances make people embarrassed. It happens automatically. It's part of the planning process.

And you must avoid the crystal ball and chain (see next section). Sometimes—actually, often—metrics go sour because assumptions have changed. Unforeseen events happened. You manage these times collaboratively, separating the effort from the results. People on your team will see that and they believe in the process, and they'll continue to contribute.

Crystal Ball and Chain

This is an answer to a question I get way too often. I call it the crystal ball and chain problem. I've run into it several times as I've introduced the planning process into a new company or organization.

People in the organization sometimes fear business planning. In the background, the fear is related to accountability and commitment. Usually they don't realize it. They state their objection like this:

> *But how can I possibly know today what's going to happen six months from now? Isn't that just a waste of time? Can't it actually be counterproductive, because it distracts us, and we spend time trying to figure out things in the future?*

I've heard this from some people who really did seem to be worried about accountability and commitment, and I've heard it from some who were stars on the team, not worried at all about their own position, but legitimately worried about the best thing for management and getting work done.

© Dusty Cline/iStock photo

The answer is that projecting future business activities isn't a ball and chain at all, because in the right planning process, the existence of the plan helps you manage effectively.

Here's a concrete example: It's September and you are developing your plan for next year, which includes an important trade show in April. You plan on that trade show and set up a budget for expenses related to that trade show. Even though it's September, you have a pretty good idea that this will happen in April.

When January rolls around, though, it turns out that the trade show that normally takes place in April will be in June this year. Does that mean the plan was wasted time? Absolutely not! It is precisely because you have a plan running that you catch the change in January, move the expenses to June, and adjust some other activities accordingly.

In this example, the plan isn't a brick wall you run into or a ball and chain that drags you down; no, it's a helpful tool, like a map or even a GPS (global positioning system) device, because it helps you keep track of priorities and manage and adjust the details as they roll into view.

It's normal for the crystal ball and chain to appear as an objection when a planning process is introduced. The solution is simply good management. The people involved in implementing the plan learn with time how regular plan review sessions help them stay on top of things, and when assumptions change, how the plan changes. Changes are discussed, nobody gets fired, and you have better management.

Business plans are always wrong, but they're still vital to good management.

The underlying idea here is directly related to the paradox I mentioned earlier: business plans are always wrong, but they're still vital to good management.

Adapted with permission from blog.timberry.com.

Set Expectations and Follow Up

I was caught on a plane once with the One Minute Manager book, by Kenneth Blanchard. I recommend that book, it's easy to read—about one short plane ride's worth—and easier to absorb. And I feel like it boils down to setting expectations with people and then following up, afterwards, with reviewing performance against expectations. You can add a lot of padding around that basic idea, but essentially it's one of those obvious ideas that's easy to say and hard to do.

TIPS &
TRAPS

HOW IRONIC IS THIS?

This is word for word from Susan Schreter's column on SeattlePI at seattlepi.com. It's from a question she received:

> I'm at the point where I have to decide if I should hire employees or farm out certain work to independent consultants. Also, please don't ask if I have a business plan because I'd rather spend my time making money than creating documents I don't have time for.

She gives a good answer.

Yogi Berra once said, "You've got to be very careful if you don't know where you're going, because you might not get there."

Unfortunately, during the past 15 years or so, business plans have morphed into a marketing tool to raise money. Entrepreneurs just don't bother to prepare them until a potential grant provider, lender, or investor requires the document as part of the selection process. It's too bad, because useful startup operating plans or business plans are built around a clear understanding of the founder's desired business destination. And this destination is not vaguely defined as "to make a lot of money" or "to be my own boss."

Entrepreneurs who say they are overwhelmed by their business rarely have a documented plan in place. Hiring, customer targeting, and other important decisions are driven by the needs of the day. It's what I call the Band-Aid approach to management. It's patch-driven rather than purpose-driven.

Your plan-as-you-go business-planning process can become a really valuable way to make that idea real, in your business, and part of your management. I've found through the years that setting expectations and following up is one of those basic principles like, say, healthy diet and regular exercise. It's easy to understand, everybody agrees that it's good to do, but not everybody manages to make it happen. It's a matter of actually doing what we know we want to, what we know we should.

Honestly, in my years as company builder, it was really hard to follow up. I think it's a natural process that you end up liking the people you work with, and, as business owner, you tend to work shoulder-to-shoulder. They aren't direct reports or sub-ordinates in your mind; they are John and Teri and Vie and Cale. They become friends.

So, in the plan-as-you-go world, that need for set-ting expectations and following up becomes part of the process. Your plan includes the metrics people need so they can know how they're doing. The core of management follow-up happens because you have a forum, a comfortable place for that hard-to-do follow-up. Your plan is built on metrics for your people, and you look at those metrics regularly. Following up gets easier.

> *In the plan-as-you-go world, that need for set-ting expectations and fol-lowing up becomes part of the process.*

Final Thought
Business Plans Are Always Wrong, But Vital

It's important enough to repeat here (from Chapter 2): all business plans are wrong, but nonetheless vital.

Paradoxical, perhaps, but still very true.

All business plans are wrong because we're human, we can't help it, we're predicting the future, and we're going to guess wrong.

But they are also vital to running a business because they help us track changes in assumptions and unexpected results in the con-text of the long-term goals of the company, long-term strategy, accountability, and, well, just about everything the plan-as-you-go business plan stands for.

A Good Business Plan Is Never Done

A good business plan is never done. If your business plan is finished, then your company is also finished.

© Matteo Natale/iStock photo

It's a lot like the legendary farmer's axe, which has had its handle changed four times and its blade changed three times, but it's still the same axe.

As your company gets used to the planning process, the business plan is always a work in progress. It gets a big refreshment every year, and a review and course correction every month.

Every so often, as business plan events come up, you spin out of your business plan a formal output piece, whether it's a pitch presentation, an elevator speech, or a full-fledged formal business plan document.

But that's not the plan, that's just output. It's the latest version. But the plan goes on, like steering, walking, dribbling, and navigation.

Don't ever wait for a plan to be done. Get going.

Index